Palgrave Advances in Sex Work Studies

This series takes a broad and interdisciplinary view of the sex industry, prioritizing transnational and intersectional work and marginalized sex workers. It seeks to center underrepresented groups such as Black, Indigenous, and other people of color; trans-feminine, transmasculine, and non-binary people; LGBTQIA+ sex workers; people with disabilities; and workers outside of the US and UK. Books in the series cover a wide range of sex industries including camming, full-service sex work in a range of contexts e.g. street-based, brothel work, and escorts), hostessing, phone sex, pornography, pro-dommes, stripping, sugar relationship, and other forms of individual sexual entrepreneurship online. They are attentive to lateral whorephobia which points to the privileges of certain forms of sex work over others and how sex workers practicing privileged forms of erotic labor often look down upon workers in more stigmatized sectors. This series also discusses criminal justice approaches to sex work and seeks titles that explore the complexities and wide range of sex worker experiences in the whorearchy to reflect the multiple positions, experiences, and perspectives of those within the sex work community.

Larissa Sandy · Petrea Nes-Iadicola ·
Daisy Matthews

Reconceptualizing Exiting and Career Development in Sex Work

Work Like Any Other

palgrave
macmillan

Larissa Sandy
School of Sociology and Social Policy
University of Nottingham
Nottingham, UK

Petrea Nes-Iadicola
Independent Researcher
Melbourne, VIC, Australia

Daisy Matthews
Nottingham Trent University
Nottingham, UK

ISSN 2731-376X ISSN 2731-3778 (electronic)
Palgrave Advances in Sex Work Studies
ISBN 978-3-032-10076-4 ISBN 978-3-032-10077-1 (eBook)
https://doi.org/10.1007/978-3-032-10077-1

Cover credit: The front cover image was created by Estelle and Taz and edited by Holly Sexton as part of a collective of Nottingham-based sex workers illustrating their sex working experiences and access to justice. The artwork was produced as part of the British Academy funded Creating Opportunities for Sex Worker Justice project in collaboration with HollyAlanaSexton Creative.

This Palgrave Macmillan imprint is published by the registered company Springer Nature Switzerland AG
The registered company address is: Gewerbestrasse 11, 6330 Cham, Switzerland

Acknowledgments This work would not have been possible without the support and participation of sex workers and sex worker advocates in Australia and Aotearoa New Zealand. We are thankful to everyone who gave generously of their time and shared their stories and experiences with us.

We would like to thank Mardi Kennedy, who first challenged us to explore this area of sex work research and programming. We would also like to thank the work of research assistants in Melbourne and Nottingham who played important roles in the larger research project this book draws on. We would like to thank Dr Joni Meenagh for her research assistance while at RMIT University, Melbourne. We also want to thank Sam Richardson-Martin and Emily Blakemore-Firth as without their research assistance in Nottingham and post-COVID, completing this book seemed like a distant possibility. We are indebted for their work in updating the literature review and wish them the best of luck with their PhD studies!

Our deepest thanks go to our families, partners, and friends who provided much-needed support during the research and writing process.

Much of the research in this book was carried out on the unceded lands of the Wurundjeri peoples of the Kulin nation, and we pay our respects to the traditional custodians of the lands on which this work was carried out.

Competing Interests The authors have no competing interests to declare that are relevant to the content of this manuscript.

Contents

Acronyms

ACT	Australian Capital Territory
CAASE	Chicago Alliance Against Sexual Exploitation
CDP	Career Development Program
CPTIC	Chicago Prostitution and Trafficking Intervention Court
CTI	Critical Time Intervention Model
NSW	New South Wales
NSWP	Network of Sex Work Projects
NT	Northern Territory
NUM	National Ugly Mugs
NZPC	New Zealand Prostitutes Collective
RhED	Resourcing Health and Education in the Sex Industry
RMIT	Royal Melbourne Institute of Technology
RUPS	*Regeling Uitstapporogramma's Prostituees* (Exit Programs for Prostitutes Scheme)
SWOP ACT	Sex Worker Outreach Program Australian Capital Territory
THDV	*Tot Heil des Volks* (For the Salvation of the People)
UK	United Kingdom
US	United States
UTS	University of Technology Sydney
UWA	University of Western Australia
VAWG	Violence against Women and Girls

List of Tables

CHAPTER 1

Introduction: A Primer to Sex Work and 'Exiting'

Abstract Sex work 'exiting' programs are behavioural change interventions designed to support people stop selling sex. In this chapter, we introduce the topics of sex work and 'exiting', tracing its transformation from early feminist discourse connected to struggles over the meaning of sex work and state attempts to regulate it, to modern-day behavioural change programs as part of sex work abolition. We begin the chapter by setting the context for this book, describing how it developed from an Australian-UK collaboration, and provide an overview of the book's key arguments. The book's overarching strategy is to reconfigure sex work as career and explore the place of 'exiting' in this, which leads us to discuss the key questions grappled with in the book as part of our effort to build new theory in this area. The chapter also provides an overview of 'exiting' and because we argue that language matters, we outline some of the key terms used in the book. After this, we discuss the research settings and methods, explore some of the ethical issues and end the chapter with an overview of the book.

Keywords Sex work · Exiting · Career · Transitions · Terminology · Research methods

L. Sandy et al., *Reconceptualizing Exiting and Career Development in Sex Work*, Palgrave Advances in Sex Work Studies,
https://doi.org/10.1007/978-3-032-10077-1_1

1.1 Introduction

The modern-era idea of 'exiting' sex work can be traced back to early feminist discourse connected to struggles over the meaning of sex work and state attempts to regulate it. In the 'traffic in women' discourse, nineteenth-century feminists like Josephine Butler cast sex workers as 'fallen women' who, as victims of male oppression, could be "brought back to womanly dignity and virtue", while social purity campaigners like Mrs. Lewis who worked in a "Magdalen Institution" in Birmingham, England, argued that through rescue and redemption sex workers could become "married and honourable wives with little children around them, living in a proper and becoming way" (Great Britain, 1871, p. 437, para. 12,852 (Butler), p. 426 para 12,552, 12, 555 (Lewis)). Here, feminist abolitionists and Christian social purity campaigners developed the idea of rescuing and rehabilitating sex workers as part of what became an international movement to end state regulation of sex work. While this movement originated in England in the 1860s, its reach was global, and the word 'abolitionism' was tied to abolitionists' understanding of their work and mission as ideologically linked with the historical struggle against transatlantic slavery (Kempadoo, 2015). In this discourse, sex work was recast as 'white slavery', with "concepts and images of black slavery … transformed to fit the case of prostitution … notably the sufferings of prostitutes in brothels and as objects of state policies" (de Vries, 2010, p. 32). In this 'traffic in women' discourse, abolitionists created the impression that sex work was little more than women's enslavement, and this led to the idea that sex work was coercive and by its very nature, forced. The slavery trope cast sex workers as victims to be rescued and worked to demonstrate and justify the need for feminist and Church involvement, and state intervention, in sex workers lives (Walkowitz, 1982).

Nowadays, the idea of rescuing and rehabilitating sex workers has been recast in sex work 'exit' programs, which are behavioural change interventions designed to support people stop selling sex. In the 1990s, 'exit' programs were developed simultaneously in Sweden and the US and had the aim of preventing the further "spread of the sex trade and its presumed negative social consequences" (Månsson & Hedin, 1999, p. 67). The first formal 'exit' program was piloted in San Francisco in 1995 as a criminal justice diversion program, and the 'exit' programs developed in Sweden were part of that country's social welfare approach to managing sex work (Wahab, 2006). 'Exit' programs now operate across the US and in Sweden (Levy & Jakobsson, 2014), Canada (Shareck et al., 2020), Denmark (Karlsson, 2024; Kofod, 2018), France (Giametta & Le Bail, 2023) where sex work is criminalised and in countries and jurisdictions where it is (or was) legalised (e.g., the Netherlands (Timmermans et al., 2019), and Melbourne, Australia (Project Respect, 2008; Resourcing Health and Education in the Sex Industry (RhED), 2013)).[1] In this way, sex work 'exiting' programs came to be part of state policies of 'caring' in welfare states, but ultimately connected with sex work regulation, they were also part of efforts to contain sex work, and thus intimately connected with the control of women's sexuality, urban populations, state borders and organised crime.

Heavily influenced by these historical and contemporary feminist debates over the meaning of sex work, Aylsworth (2020) argues that modern-day understandings of sex work have come to be shaped by ideas about 'participation', or what it means to do sex work and 'non-participation', or what it means to no longer sex work. These ideas about sex work and 'exiting' came into public consciousness through the framing of sex work as a form of violence against women that women needed help to escape from and for law enforcement, containment and control. But there are issues with this framing, as the idea of being 'involved in' or 'exited from' sex work has produced one-dimensional frameworks for conceptualising sex work participation, which is the subject of this book. Building on pioneering research carried out by Bowen (2021) exploring people's engagement in sex work that cuts across sex work and non-sex work employment, this book is among the first to articulate a complex redefinition of 'exiting' based on grounded observations and local realities. Noticeable in our book is the centrality of sex workers voices and experiences, which have largely been silenced in research and analysis.

The book was initially inspired by research carried out by Larissa Sandy and Petrea Nes-Iadicola as part of an Australian-based study exploring best practice in 'exiting' programs (Sandy et al., 2019a, b). Here, we carried out an evidence review of 'exiting' programs with Joni Meenagh for a Melbourne-based sex worker support program providing transitioning services created in part due to the stigma people confronted

[1] The Victorian Government passed the *Sex Work Decriminalisation Act* in 2022 which led to the decriminalisation of sex work in that Australian state.

when they wanted to leave sex work. At the time Sandy developed the project, there was a renewed emphasis on 'exiting' programs in the state of Victoria, Australia, with the government providing significant financial support for the development of new programs and ongoing funding for existing ones. For example, the 2017–18 state budget provided an additional AU$4 million over four years to RhED for the Pathways program (Parliament of Victoria, 2017). In the same financial year, Project Respect also received funding to develop the Breaking Barriers: Enhancing Employment Pathways program and the City of Port Phillip provided funding to St Kilda Gatehouse for the Greeves St. project, which is a program assisting street-based sex workers to leave sex work (State of Victoria, 2018; City of Port Phillip, n.d.).

Given the growing public interest, we were keen to explore the research on 'exiting' programs, particularly as the government was considering sex work decriminalisation and 'exiting' programs were a key policy issue. Here, our research set out to reposition 'exiting' by exploring the practice through the prism of decriminalisation and a labour framework: what would this look like, and how would services change as a result—or indeed, would they be needed? Daisy Matthews joined the book through her work on a violence prevention program with Larissa Sandy and Sam Richardson-Martin at a Nottingham-based sex worker support agency in the United Kingdom (UK). Matthews' involvement brought an understanding and deeper appreciation of the Swedish Model, which has come to shape most debates about sex work regulation and law reform in the UK. The understanding that developed through working together was that 'exiting' was unable to account for the diversity in employment in sex work and did little to aid an appreciation of how sex workers themselves made sense of and understood their working lives. In our discussions, we began to see how 'exiting' studies were part of the long history of attempts to rescue and rehabilitate sex workers (mostly from themselves) and silence dissenting voices, which led us to start documenting the exclusion of sex workers in 'exiting' research and analyses. Our shared conceptualisation of the problem offered an alternative perspective to the abolitionist, mostly Western radical feminist view dominating international debates on sex work. Through this, we came to realise that we were articulating a complex redefinition of sex work and 'exiting' based on grounded research and understanding sex workers' complex and multifaceted experiences, which is a perspective we set out to make visible in the book.

This book documents sex work 'exiting' not as sex workers needing to stop doing sex work, but as part of sex work careers, analysed from the lives, agency, rights, voices and views of diverse peoples engaged in sex work. It sheds new light on everyday working circumstances, popular discourses and theorisations, national policies and grassroot struggles for change and repositioning. More than that, by conceptualising the issue from sex workers' diverse and varied views and perspectives, or the ground up, the book links theory and practice in ways overlooked in 'exiting' research. The analyses undertaken are sex worker-centred, which offers a unique vantage point from which we can understand the issue and contribute to its reformulation in a labour and rights framework and approach by using the lens of sex work as career.

As a result, the book is among the first to comprehensively examine the consequences of this controversial area of service provision, often linked with views about sex work as harmful and sex workers as victims. We argue that it is important to critique and reposition this area of sex work research as, while 'exiting' programs claim to provide supportive routes out of sex work, Gaynor and Gifford (2022) note how they often work to reconfigure and reinforce the exclusion of sex workers from society. The book, then, is part of our mutual exploration and theorisation of sex work as labour, in which we examine how sex work can be conceptualised as career and where 'exiting' may or may not fit with sex worker life narratives and working experiences. We do this, however, while also challenging the discourse surrounding sex work as categorisations of 'involved' and 'exited', and, as Aylsworth (2020) suggests, the widespread view of these categories as distinct and stable. In this way, we see this book as contributing to efforts to reconceptualise sex work as work and career, for like Gilmour, we agree that to recognise the "diversity of sex work careers and the broader socio-economic forces that shape choices, sex work needs to be more clearly reconfigured within a career framework" (2020, p. 298). This is part of our original contribution to critical engagement with the concept of career in 'exiting' and sex work studies.

Our overarching strategy is, to reconfigure sex work as career, and in doing this, we can unpack the dominant frameworks shaping how 'exiting' is conceptualised and explore alternatives explore alternatives to better understand sex workers' perspectives and thoughts on this area of service provision. Consequently, the book presents new analyses tracing the research evidence on ‘exiting’ programs and evaluating program effectiveness, particularly in consideration of different legislative contexts and models of good practice. The central objective driving the book is to understand sex workers lived realities, which leads to our continual foregrounding of sex workers’ lives and experiences. We were particularly interested in learning about how sex workers navigated leaving sex work through formal programs and informal processes, leading to focused discussion of sex workers experiences with ‘exiting’ from a rarely considered labour and work perspective. In addressing a gap in research, we were keen to explore how sex workers and allies perceived ‘exiting’, and how they understood and made sense of this area of service provision, which is documented, perhaps for the first time in this book. In exploring the link between theory and praxis, we set out to better understand how theories on sex work ‘exiting’ were able to account for sex workers’ experiences and views. This leads us to in-depth discussion of the ways in which these theories could be adapted or modified to address the complexities of workers’ lived experiences and, eventually, to developing an alternative framework that is more inclusive and based on sex workers own understandings of sex work as career. Through this work, the book presents a new framing of sex work ‘exiting’ as career development, and we argue, a paradigm shift more apt at capturing sex workers’ lived experiences, with the potential to radically change theoretical understandings of the issue and transform policy and practice.

In short, the book grapples with the question of how to conceptualise and respond to ‘exiting’. In answering this question, we explore ideas about gender equality, exploitation, sex work regulation and the regulation of sexuality to self-determination, working conditions, socioeconomic disparities and careers in sex work. We put forward our ideas for reconceptualising ‘exiting’ sex work as career and present our reasons for what we see is a much-needed paradigm change. This leads to our development of a new theory centred on how and where ‘exiting’ may or may not fit with sex workers narratives and experiences and do so to challenge dominant discourse and theorisations favouring sex work as deviance and criminalising approaches. Our aim here is to show how these dominant frameworks obscure understanding labour rights and thus perpetuate stigma and discrimination and cause harm. However, we also hope that this new theorisation leads to greater social acceptance of sex work as work and changes in policy and practice. Ultimately, we hope the book reveals the paradox of ‘exiting’. Although this area of programming claims to help workers, it is achieved at the cost of further compounding marginalisation and reinforcing harms, while simultaneously acting as a domain of oppression in sex workers' lives.

1.2 Note on Terminology

Language matters when we talk about sex work (Stella, 2013), and so there are a few key terms used in this book that we want to define. We do not use the terms 'sex work' and 'prostitution' interchangeably as the terms are not interchangeable. The term 'sex work' sees sex work as work and recognises people providing sexual services as workers. 'Prostitution' and 'prostitute' carry the idea of criminality and immorality and are terms tied to the discipline and control of certain groups of women. Sex work was a term developed by sex workers to describe and explain the reality of their lives and work (Leigh, 1997). When we use the term 'sex work', this means understanding sex work from the perspective of sex workers' lived experiences, and it is a term used by sex workers themselves. Pitcher notes that understanding sex work as work, and using this terminology, does not mean we cannot consider "exploitation or interrelated issues such as labour market segregation and relative power and disadvantage" (2015, p. 113). We also use this term as it reflects the diversity within the sex work community and a "rights-affirming, non-judgemental, inclusive terminology... to describe the people, activities, and arrangements in sex work" (Network of Sex Work Projects (NSWP), 2024, p. 2).

'Prostitution' is an archaic term, and we see this as reinforcing stigma and discrimination around sex work and sex workers. The root meaning of the term means 'to offer publicly' or 'exposed publicly' and was drawn from ancient Roman social practices dictating that 'prostitute women' appeared in public with their faces uncovered, unlike female citizens (Perkins, 1991). This was one of the many infringements of sex workers' rights imposed by the state and a method of status differentiation used to separate sex workers from 'respectable women' (McGinn, 2003). The Latin roots of the term 'prostitute' are connected to publicly exposing "someone to shame and rebuke", and as such it is a dysphemism for sex work (Büschi, 2014, p. 726). In English law, the term 'common prostitute' was introduced in the *Vagrancy Act* (1824) and *Street Offences Act* (1959), and it not only made street-based sex work illegal but was a gendered term that could only be applied to women (Jerrard, 1995). While subsequent legislation eliminated the use of 'common prostitute', terms like 'prostitute' and 'prostitution' are part of the stigmatising language surrounding sex work. Where studies cited in the book have used problematic language, we have made a choice to retain this language. This is because it helps to show that the works we are discussing may not necessarily represent the voices and views of all sex workers.

In this book, we define sex work as the provision of sexual services for payment (cash or in kind), with the practice involving more formal commercial exchanges also known as 'direct' services (e.g., street, brothel, massage and escort work), and 'non-direct' services (e.g., erotic dancing, strip shows, web camming and phone sex) (Sanders et al., 2009). Sex workers include female, male, trans and gender diverse adults and young people who receive money or goods in exchange for sexual services (UNAIDS, 2012). There are sex workers who do and do not have in-person contact with clients, with the term 'full-service' used to refer to people who provide in-person sex services (it is interesting to note that most research is with full-service sex workers) (Sawicki et al., 2019). Sex work takes place in a variety of locations, ranging from brothels, massage parlours and relaxation centres (or similar dedicated establishments) to clubs, strip clubs, hotels, private homes, bars, restaurants, parks and the streets as well as online, and it may be recognisable or hidden (Sanders et al., 2009). It is important to recognise the many different and varied forms of sex work, because this often shapes what buying and selling sex means and how and where it is sold.

We do not assume that all people doing sex work want to 'exit', nor do we endorse such views or perspectives. Like O'Neill and Campbell, we also argue for "complex, nuanced, non-polarised analyses and understandings of people's movement into and out of sex work" (2010, p. 186). In this book, we avoid using the term 'exit' uncritically and prefer terms like transitioning, leaving sex work or career development. Ultimately, we agree with Law's (2013) point that the term 'exiting' is disrespectful because it simplifies the diverse employment experiences within sex work. For these reasons, we use 'exiting' to distance ourselves from the term and show that we do not endorse its use or meaning in sex work research as it is inappropriate.

1.3 Methods

The exploratory nature of this project lent itself to a qualitative research design, and, in answering the book's questions, we felt that a few methods were necessary. This is because the questions we posed required us to explore the many different dimensions of the issue. We also hoped that using more than one method would result in us developing a more nuanced understanding of 'exiting' and thus enhance the depth, breadth and validity of our findings by allowing us to triangulate data and gain a more comprehensive understanding. Additionally, by using a few methods we could mitigate against the weakness inherent in using one single method. Our methods included a narrative literature review, in-depth interviews and case studies, and in this section, we provide detail on each of these methods and data analysis.

1.3.1 Literature Review

The literature review presented in this book is a narrative summary review that set out to explore 'exiting' and 'exiting' programs in sex work research. As well as providing an academic foundation for the research presented here, this review also aimed to document sex workers' experiences and map existing programs to provide case studies of good practice. In 2018, Meenagh, Nes-Iadicola and Sandy conducted database and directed searches for academic and grey literature reporting on research from the last fifteen years (2002–2017) and the searches were updated in 2024 by Matthews, supported by Sam Richardson-Martin and Emily Blakemore-Firth. The review recounts and describes existing approaches in 'exiting', with the findings focusing on theoretical framings, program design and approaches, the impact of different legislative contexts and sex workers' experiences of 'exiting'. The review is an interpretative account critically reflecting on the state of the field and, by drawing out the assumptions on which these programs are based, highlights ideological issues and key flaws in this area of service provision. It also explored best practices in this area, using a best practice framework developed by Sandy and Nes-Iadicola, through which we first began developing and discussing the idea of career development in sex work (Sandy et al., 2019b). The outcomes of this aspect of the narrative review establishing good practice are presented as case studies in this book.

1.3.2 Case Studies

We use case studies in the book to explain, describe and explore 'exiting' and transitioning in the everyday contexts in which it occurs (Yin, 2014). The case studies were led by Nes-Iadicola as part of a global review of 'exiting' programs (Sandy et al., 2019a). These case studies are featured in Chapters 3 and 6. We were attracted to this method as it allowed for an in-depth, contextual analysis of issues in real-word settings and deeper examination of programs. Here, we aimed to understand how interventions were being implemented on the ground, what gaps there were in service delivery and why one intervention might be chosen over another (Crowe et al., 2011). In doing this, we were wanting to develop and refine theories about sex work and 'exiting' and how they were applied in practice while also highlighting key assumptions and documenting promising (and not so promising) practice.

As introduced above, the case studies were identified from the literature review through research studies reporting on programs complemented by a desk-based online search via Google with the key words: sex work transitioning programs/programmes; sex work exiting programs/programmes; sex work career development; prostitution exiting programs/programmes; diversion programs/programmes; sex work organisations/organizations; and prostitute organisations/organizations. In addition to using these search terms, Nes-Iadicola contacted the UK-based Sex Work Research Hub to find out about programs in the UK and Canada, and where the contact details were available, we contacted each individual organisation to enquire whether they had an 'exiting' or transitioning program, and if so, whether they could provide any information. The search strategy was not meant to be exhaustive, rather we aimed to provide a microcosm of the types of programs focusing on transitioning/career development/'exiting' globally. Using these methods, we identified a significant number of programs in the United States (US); however, most had similar models based on a sex work as exploitation framework and were delivered as diversion programs. As such, we focused on four key US-based programs when undertaking the analysis presented in the book as it was beyond our ability to include all US-based programs. The case studies presented in the book are descriptive, and we use them to investigate current and former programs from a 'best practice' perspective (described in data analysis below), answer questions about program design and implementation and exploratory, where we wanted to understand the potential barriers and challenges and identify good practice.

The case studies chosen for presentation here are drawn from across the world to provide variety in context and settings and explore complexity, particularly in light of sex work regulation and how this shapes program delivery and workers' experiences. Case study analysis and write up was carried out by Matthews, Nes-Iadicola and Sandy, and each case study is a "bounded context" in that it presents an in-depth study of a particular program or approach (Miles & Huberman, 2019, p. 25; Green & Thorogood, 2009). The case studies adopt a critical (questioning assumptions) and interpretivist (understanding individual and shared meanings and experiences) approach. We developed this approach to draw on a critical, reflective perspective that takes the wider social and political environment shaping the case into account (Crowe et al., 2011; Doolin, 1998).

1.3.3 In-Depth Interviews

Australia and Aotearoa New Zealand were selected as the interviewing locations as the sex work regulatory landscape ranged from criminalisation to legalisation and decriminalisation. In Australia, sex work is regulated by the different state and territory governments meaning there is no national framework, with each jurisdiction setting the regulatory approach. This includes licensing in the Australian Capital Territory, decriminalisation in New South Wales and criminalisation in South Australia, Tasmania and Western Australia. Street-based sex work is illegal in these three states and tends to be heavily policed, but private work is legal. Partial criminalisation in Tasmania and Western Australia means that, while brothel and agency work is legal in Western Australia, it is illegal to own or operate a brothel, and it is legal for one or two workers to work together in Tasmania. Recent legislative change saw the Northern Territory, Victoria and Queensland shift from licensing to decriminalisation in 2019, 2022 and 2024, respectively. Aotearoa New Zealand operates a national decriminalisation policy. Australia and Aotearoa New Zealand offered something unique, and we saw this as a way for us to speak about the different legislative contexts, thereby giving the book global relevance and currency. It also allowed us to talk about sex work in decriminalised settings and thus fill a gap in the regulatory literature which mostly centres on criminalisation. We also selected these locations to fill a significant gap in research as no research on 'exiting' had been carried out in Australia and Aotearoa New Zealand. These interview data are featured in Chapters 4 and 6.

The interviews in the book were led by Sandy as part of exploratory work into best practices in 'exiting' programs (Sandy et al., 2019b). The research received approval from RMIT University's College of Design and Social Context Human Ethics Advisory Network in 2017. Twenty-one in-depth interviews were carried out (totalling 28 individual interviewees) with peer and non-peer organisations that provided 'exiting' or transitioning services or programs across Australia and Aotearoa New Zealand between 21 December 2017 and 12 March 2018. Based on the findings from these interviews, 'peer' is defined as a person with a lived experience of sex work, or as "people who identify as sex workers and carry the stigma associated with that" (Interview with Ava). A peer organisation or peer-based organisation is where members of an affected community develop and implement harm reduction strategies for and with their peers, while a non-peer organisation provides services to members of an affected community and is staffed by a blend of peers and non-peers. Peer-led programs are a key characteristic of service provision in Australia, with most state or territory governments providing funding to peer-led support services; however, historically this has not been the case for all states and territories, and we thought it important to recognise community governance and ownership and acknowledge this in the book.

The interviews aimed to document program development and other activities undertaken in Australia and Aotearoa New Zealand as the earlier literature review identified a significant gap with most of this information not published or publicly available. The purpose of the interviews, then, was to gain an updated understanding of 'exiting' or transitioning programs, types of services, methods of delivery and identification of best practice. We also saw interviews as a way to understand sex workers' perspectives of 'exiting' and how they made sense of and understood this area of service provision as this was a key gap identified in the literature review.

The in-depth interviews were carried out by Sandy and Meenagh and allowed for exploration of participants' own experiences and meaning making, with participants interviewed about their experiences of service delivery, understandings of transitioning and 'exiting' and best practice (Hesse-Biber, 2014; Maynes et al., 2012). We employed narrative-based principles and interviewing techniques, where the interview was seen as a collaborative creation produced by both interviewer and interviewee

(Kennedy et al., 2023; Presser & Sandberg, 2015). We were keen to use narrative frameworks and interviewing techniques as it seeks to explore harm and oppression and resistances to this, while inviting us to develop a reflexive stance in our research (Presser & Sandberg, 2019). We also wanted to see if narrative frameworks could help in shifting public stories about 'exiting' and deconstructing frameworks and ideologies. We saw this as important in the context of sex work law reform, particularly with sex work decriminalisation in Australia and stalled law reform efforts elsewhere (e.g., the UK), and countering prevailing ideas about sex work as harmful and sex workers as victims in need of rescue. This is because narrative frameworks are powerful tools in influencing how people understand and think about an issue and the actions they then think societies and governments should take (Moniz et al., 2023). We selected this method for its ability to tap into narratives that could shape public opinion, create social change and influence policy developed from sex workers' needs. In setting out to achieve this, we made sure the interview schedule was designed to prompt concrete stories in a non-directive way wherein the researcher was framed as an essential part of the dynamic (Gubrium & Holstein, 2012; Hollway & Jefferson, 1997). This means we did not employ the traditional 'question-and-answer' format structured around 'why' questions but rather designed the interview schedule to elicit narratives from participants (Hollway & Jefferson, 1997). Like in-depth interviewing, this method also prioritises building rapport while actively engaging with participants, with the idea being to guide the conversation to topics participants see as important, while also using their own language, perceptions and understandings to share experiences (Jovchelovitch & Bauer, 2000; Maynes et al., 2012). Twenty-one interviews were carried out (16 one-on-one interviews and 5 small group interviews) and ranged from 60 to 150 minutes. Some interviews were face-to-face, by phone, or Skype and recorded with participant permission.

1.3.3.1 Research Participants

Interview participants were recruited from organisations working with sex workers across Australia and Aotearoa New Zealand. Smith and Pitts (2007) discuss researching with marginalised communities and note that convenience sampling is an appropriate technique to use in research with hard-to-reach and marginalised populations. In recognising this, Sandy used convenience sampling in the interviews, in which 28 people agreed to take part. As we used convenience sampling, the sample was not statistically representative but as a qualitative project, our research did not set out to be representative; rather, we aimed to gain a deeper understanding of participants' experiences (Barbour, 2001; Caelli et al., 2003). Care was taken to ensure there was a broad variety of participants to capture diversity and complexity as the aim of the work was to explore and gain insight into the experiences and perspectives of sex workers and advocates, and a full list of interview participants is included in Table 1.1.

In research, sex workers are often characterised as 'vulnerable', however, sometimes this term is used "not as an adjective but rather to refer to a 'class' of sex workers", for example, this is something we are noticing with increased use of the term 'survival sex work/survival sex workers' (Stella, 2013, p. 3). In sex work research, 'survival sex' can be used to divide sex workers in a way that works to legitimise the decisions of some workers and not others as 'survival sex workers' are sometimes seen as "not strong or not capable of making the best decisions for themselves" (Stella, 2013, p. 3). This distinction also has ramifications in terms of the conflation of sex work and trafficking and the rise of safeguarding and vulnerability frameworks wherein 'survival sex workers' are labelled as victims of sexual exploitation or trafficking (Hanks, 2022; Sandy, 2014). Finally, the way 'vulnerability' is conceptualised in sex work research can sometimes translate into an inability to account for exclusion because of systemic oppression and legal and socioeconomic contexts (NSWP, 2024). 'Vulnerable' can lead to a framing that ignores how sex workers are vulnerable because of sex work laws and socioeconomic conditions as well as lacking protections and rights, which needs to be considered in ethical research with sex workers (Stella, 2013).

Research participants can be prone to harm or exploitation, and we need to address this in projects, but as Meek Lange, Rogers and Dodds note we need to respond to vulnerability in a way that "avoids stereotyping and paternalism and is consistent with the principle of respect for individual autonomy" (2013, p. 340). In striking a balance between protection and participation rights, participants had the option of being named in the research or allocated a pseudonym to protect their identities. Participants who indicated a preference to be identified by their known name are identified as such in this book. Participating programs and/or organisations that agreed to be identified are included in Table 1.1, along with basic information on participants.

Table 1.1 Participant characteristics

Pseudonym/legal name	*Location*	*Role*	*Organisation*
Abigail		Frontline service provider	
Ahi Wi-Hongi	Wellington, Aotearoa New Zealand	Community Liaison	New Zealand Prostitutes Collective (NZPC)
Alison		Frontline service provider	
Amelia		Frontline service provider	
Ava		Frontline service provider	
Catherine Healy	Wellington, Aotearoa New Zealand	National Coordinator	NZPC
Catriona Hodgson	Melbourne, Australia	Health Education Coordinator	Resourcing Health and Education in the Sex Industry (RhED)
Cecilia		Frontline service provider	
Charlotte		Frontline service provider	
Christina Hotka	Melbourne, Australia	Pathways Worker	Pathways Program, RhED
Emma		Frontline service provider	
Gabby Skelsey	Melbourne, Australia	Health Educator	RhED
Georgie		Frontline service provider	
Jane Green	Melbourne, Australia	Spokesperson	Vixen Collective
Jill Martin	Melbourne, Australia	Health Educator	RhED
Jules Kim	Sydney, Australia	CEO	Scarlet Alliance
Lexxie Jury	Canberra, Australia	Outreach Coordinator	Sex Worker Outreach Program (SWOP) ACT
Lisa		Frontline service provider	
Mandy Bliss	Brisbane & Townsville, Australia	Career Development Peer Worker	Career Development Program, Respect Inc
Mia		Frontline service provider	

(continued)

Table 1.1 (continued)

Pseudonym/legal name	*Location*	*Role*	*Organisation*
Michael		Frontline service provider	
Olivia		Frontline service provider	
P.G. Macioti	Sydney, Melbourne & Perth, Australia	Former Outreach Coordinator & Postdoctoral Fellow	Hydra e.V, Germany and University of Technology Sydney (UTS) and University of Western Australia (UWA)
Rachel Reilly	Melbourne, Australia	Executive Director	Project Respect
Sally Boothby	Melbourne, Australia	Criminal Justice Worker	Arrest Referral Program, RhED
Sarah		Frontline service provider	
Sophia		Frontline service provider	
Tanya Morrison	Auckland, Aotearoa New Zealand	Community Liaison	NZPC

Research participants and organisations have been named with informed, written consent, as per RMIT University Ethics Approval. People and organisations that took part in the research but did not wish to be identified are included in this list, but only basic details have been included. Some participants were happy for their organisation to be named but wished to remain personally anonymous and, to protect their identity, we have not linked their pseudonym with the organisation or geographical location. Table 1.1 does not contain the complete list of participating organisations as some participants did not want the organisation they were based at to be identified. Pseudonyms have been used for all participants who did not wish to be identified. We felt that taking this approach was important in research where a labelling conception of 'vulnerability' can result in people being labelled as vulnerable simply because they belong to a subpopulation (Luna, 2009). Protecting against vulnerability is at the core of research ethics, and while certain ethics requirements about protection are well intentioned, as Daley (2015) argues, this may have unintended consequences, with the need to protect participants overriding concerns about enabling participation and a person's right to give voice and ultimately, their self-determination (see also Loomes, 2018). We feel that it is essential for researchers working with people who are often labelled as 'vulnerable' to recognise the importance of marginalised people having the right to be represented in research in a way that respects their individual and collective rights and autonomy, while also protecting against potential harms.

Interviews were transcribed verbatim, and either anonymised incorporating a participant's pseudonym or identified. For participants wishing to remain anonymous, transcripts were de-identified, and pseudonyms used to further protect confidentiality of participation. Although these steps were taken to protect confidentiality, there is a chance that people familiar with people working in the sector might be able to guess the identity of individual people. Participants were informed of this possibility as part of the informed consent process. All participants received a copy of the transcript to edit and check for accuracy. The return of transcripts acted as a form of participant validation, and while the methods literature largely focuses on debates about how this practice may affect data quality, we felt that returning transcripts for participant review was of vital importance in sensitive research. While transcript return was a way to check data and findings with participants and establish credibility (Lincoln & Guba, 1985; Varpio et al., 2017), another key reason we did this was in implementing a feminist research ethic and breaking down asymmetrical power relations (Burgess-Proctor, 2015). We also saw this as a practice recognising the agency of participants and offering some control over the use of sensitive data, which we felt was important in our research (Rowlands, 2021). Participant validation of transcripts was key in providing assurance about and encouraging active involvement in research and fostering more respectful, community-responsive research (Neufeld et al., 2019).

1.3.4 Data Analysis

Sandy led the analysis of interview data with Meenagh and Nes-Iadicola. Interviews were analysed using reflexive thematic analysis, which places emphasis on the reflexivity of the researcher and theoretical flexibility while being guided by the research questions (Braun & Clarke, 2019).

As Braun and Clarke (2021a) suggest, this led to the development of meaningful, conceptually driven themes rather than simplistic categories. Data analysis followed the six recursive and iterative phases of analysis and construction of themes, which allowed themes to emerge from the data. Reflexive thematic analysis recognises that this process is also mediated by the researchers, and as such, it was essential to understand and reflect on our assumptions and values, and how this shaped and delimited the coding (Braun & Clarke, 2021b). The major themes identified during reflexive thematic analysis are discussed throughout the book.

Nes-Iadicola led the analysis of 'exiting' programs with Matthews and Sandy. Case studies were analysed using critical content analysis and evaluated in terms of whether the programs fit examples of best practice, promising practice or emerging practice in 'exiting' programs. In establishing best, promising, or emerging practice in 'exiting' programs, Sandy and Nes-Iadicola developed analytical criteria for determining this, in addition to developing a framework for establishing best practice in sex work programs based on a review of the literature complemented by interview data. Table 1.2 lists the analytical criteria we developed to guide our global review of 'exiting' programs. In each case study presented in the book, we include a short description of these categorisations and our rationale for exclusion/inclusion as promising or best practice along with a brief description of the program.

Table 1.2 Evaluation framework for 'exiting' program analysis

Exclusion criteria used for ruling out best practice in 'exit' programs	*Exclusion criteria used for ruling out promising practice in 'exit' programs*	*Inclusion criteria used for establishing best practice in sex work programming*
Grey literature only (no peer-reviewed research)	No basis in theories, standards or evidence	Sex work as work
No basis in theories, standards or evidence	Limited quality of evidence	Rights-based approach & community empowerment framework
Implemented only once		Peer driven (sex worker-led)
Low size of impact		Peer engagement and outreach
Moderate quality of evidence in evaluations		

In understanding best, promising and emerging practice, we define best practice as an intervention, method, or technique shown to be effective through rigorous scientific research (ideally conducted by independent researchers) and replicated elsewhere (e.g., across several cases or examples) (Canadian Homelessness Research Network (CHRN), 2013). It is an intervention, program, service, strategy, or policy that, through multiple implementations, has repeatedly demonstrated a positive impact on the outcomes and objectives of the intervention and given the evidence, it is seen as the most suitable one for a particular situation or context (Fazal et al., 2017). Promising practice is defined as an intervention, program, service, strategy, or policy that shows potential (e.g., promise) for developing into best practice (Fazal et al., 2017). There is some evidence (needs to be of a suitable quality) to demonstrate the practice is effective at achieving a specific aim or outcome that is consistent with program objectives (CHRN, 2013). While promising practices demonstrate effectiveness through research (and the research is sound), there may not be enough evidence for it to be considered best practice, or it may be that the practice is in the earlier stages of implementation (Fazal et al., 2017). Emerging practice refers to interventions that are innovative and new and hold promise based on some level of evidence of effectiveness; however, this may not be research-based or enough to be considered promising or best practice (CHRN, 2013). This may be because the intervention is new and there has not been enough time to conduct research.

These definitions were essential in guiding our analysis of different programs as, while many programs may make claims to promising or best practice, there was a lot of variation in the quality and rigour of research and evidence used to back these claims. As these definitions make clear, the determining factor we used for making a claim of best or promising practice was evidence. This evidence can be in the form of systematic reviews (meta-analyses and meta-syntheses) in addition to randomised control trials, often considered 'gold star' but having some ethical drawbacks, and quasi-experimental studies (CHRN, 2013; Fazal et al., 2017). As this is an emerging area of research and program work, we considered summative literature reviews and case studies containing evidence of effectiveness as a way to determine emerging and promising practice (CHRN, 2013; Powell & Sandy, 2015). Mayhew and Mossman (2007, p. 30) highlight that it is quite difficult to establish 'best practice' as opposed to 'what works'. In addressing this criticism, we have defined 'best practice', 'promising practice' and 'emerging practice', and developed a clear set of evaluation criteria we then used to determine this (see Table 1.2 above). Almost all of the programs we reviewed failed to meet the criteria for best and promising practice, but a few met the criteria for emerging practice. Most programs did not meet the criteria for promising practice largely due to the quality of evidence available.

1.4 Overview of the Book

This book, then, focuses on a rearticulation of 'exiting' discourse in mainly feminist and abolitionist (and abolitionist feminist) definitions since the 1980s. It draws attention away from state imperatives for exercising greater control over sex workers, some of whom are part of the urban poor and migrant and marginalised communities, recentring this on the needs, agency and rights of diverse sex workers.

Chapter 2, *Exiting Assumptions*, addresses the main problems with current conceptualisations of 'exiting' and begins to propose new ways forward. In this chapter, we critically discuss the hegemonic 'exiting' discourse and point to the main theories framing 'exiting', to unpack and unravel the assumptions on which they are based. 'Exiting', we note, leads to narrow framings that shape ideas of sex work as something someone is either 'in' or 'out' of, and rests upon the idea of sex work being a harmful activity people are trapped in. Through this framing sex workers are constructed as victims who need to be rescued, and it is this theoretical landscape of 'exiting' that harms sex workers.

Chapter 3 explores crimino-legal responses and takes stock of contemporary 'exiting' interventions, or as we have titled it, *The Good, The Bad and The Ugly*. In evaluating the programs resulting from 'exiting' frameworks explored in Chapter 2, we use case studies to present and explore the issues with some of the more problematic framings elaborated on in that chapter. In this chapter, we confront the legacy of the conflation of sex work with violence against women. We show how the combination of abolitionist feminist perspectives, conservative Christian sexuality morality and sex-negative legal approaches have influenced sex work laws and policies, culminating in its criminalisation and the development of 'exiting' programs. Here we highlight how the operation of abolitionist ideology in sex work policy and programs can result in greater harms to sex workers through an anti-sex work approach and denial of workers' rights. In this chapter, we demonstrate some of the quite profound implications for sex workers' health and well-being and safety. In our analysis, we set the legislative framework as the bounded context for program analysis, and do so to highlight how these programs and framings are linked with morality politics that frames sex workers as criminal and/or vulnerable and in need of intervention and protection. We do this to encourage academics, practitioners and policy makers to develop more realistic and appropriate understandings and interventions. Combined, these two chapters set out the significance of sex worker inclusion in any attempt to regulate their lives and work—*nothing about us, without us*—and critique the systemic violence that takes place in the name of sex work regulation. We do need to give a warning as these chapters contain content that may be triggering and offensive as it includes whorephobic work.

Chapter 4, *Changing the Narrative*, presents grounded research with sex workers and explores their lived realities. For perhaps the first time in publication, it introduces sex worker and advocate perspectives of 'exiting' highlighting issues with 'exiting' frameworks and ideologies that perpetuate sex work stigma. As the title suggests, this chapter asks us to consider language and the impact of 'exiting' on sex work stigma. In this chapter, we use interview data to explore sex workers' resistance to 'exiting' and highlight the problematic framings of respectability that underpin the practice. Through interview data, we reveal the paradox of 'exiting', namely, while these programs may be needed because of sex work stigma, 'exiting' itself perpetuates stigma. It is in this chapter that we show the pressing need to reconceptualise 'exiting'—put simply, it is important that we change the narrative as our analyses highlight the problematic framings of respectability in 'exiting' and show how this acts as a domain of oppression in sex workers' lives.

Chapter 5, *Beyond the Binary*, demonstrates the need for reframing as this chapter considers the specific ways in which sex workers engage with 'exiting' in their working lives. This chapter explores sex workers' experiences with leaving sex work, which can include engaging in a formal 'exiting' program or more informal approaches. In this chapter, we draw on existing research to create a picture of how sex workers 'exit', or disengage with the sex industry, or not. Using a labour framework, the chapter highlights the misalignment of sex workers diverse practices and experiences and allows us to begin considering ideas about career development and progression in sex work.

Chapter 6, *Careers in Sex Work*, traces the emergence of grassroots efforts to reconceptualise 'exiting' as career development through programs developed by and for sex workers. This chapter discusses how the varied ideas and assumptions about sex work and 'exiting' are being transformed through a collective desire to find clear, workable, sex worker-centred solutions to the issue, which we hope this book contributes to. The chapter documents the work undertaken to gain clarity about 'exiting' and practices in the sector, leading to the creation of new programs informed by the idea of career development and progressions, and the new model for understanding sex work and 'exiting' presented in this book. The chapter shows how an open, interactive and participatory process can produce new shared definitions and understandings that offer different ways of thinking about sex work and 'exiting'. Chapters 4, 5 and 6 richly demonstrate and further ground our earlier analyses of 'exiting', stressing the very complicated intersections of gender, race, sexuality and class. It also proposes alternative ways of thinking about 'exiting' and demonstrates the value and importance of researching *with* sex workers, rather than 'on' sex work (Connelly & Sanders, 2020).

Ultimately, the book's conclusion, and our main thesis, urges us to carefully consider the situation of many sex workers across the world and makes a compelling case for the urgent need to construct more accurate definitions and concepts and develop laws, policies and interventions that empower and liberate sex workers and see sex work as real work. Drawing on Connelly and Sanders' (2020) work, this book is part of broader attempts to disrupt the boundaries that exist between the academe and activism and show why it matters. We see this as part of our ongoing efforts to disrupt and challenge harmful narratives about sex work and here, the book's significance lies in setting out a new way of thinking about 'exiting' and this, we hope, will be a powerful challenge of the status quo.

References

Aylsworth, L. (2020). *Rethinking 'involvement' in sex work: Examining sex workers relationship with sex work* [doctoral dissertation, University of Alberta]. *ERA*. https://era.library.ualberta.ca/items/678db113-4e1a-45d7-b338-36969ed2f358

Barbour, R. (2001). Checklists for improving rigour in qualitative research: A case of the tail wagging the dog? *British Medical Journal, 322*(7294), 1115–1117. https://doi.org/10.1136/bmj.322.7294.1115
Bowen, R. (2021). *Work, money and duality: Trading sex as a side hustle*. Bristol University Press.
Braun, V., & Clarke, V. (2021a). To saturate or not to saturate? Questioning data saturation as a useful concept for thematic analysis and sample-size rationale. *Qualitative Research in Sport, Exercise and Health, 13*, 201–216. https://doi.org/10.1080/2159676X.2019.1704846
Braun, V., & Clarke, V. (2021b). Can I use TA? Should I use TA? Should I not use TA? Comparing reflexive thematic analysis and other pattern-based qualitative analytical approaches. *Counselling & Psychotherapy Research, 21*, 37–42. https://doi.org/10.1002/capr.12360
Braun, V., & Clarke, V. (2019). Reflecting on reflexive thematic analysis. *Qualitative Research in Sport, Exercise & Health, 11*, 589–597. https://doi.org/10.1080/2159676X.2019.1628806
Burgess-Proctor, A. (2015). Methodological and ethical issues in feminist research with abused women: Reflections on participants' vulnerability and empowerment. *Women's Studies International Forum, 48*, 124–134. https://doi.org/10.1016/j.wsif.2014.10.014
Büschi, E. (2014). Sex work and violence: Focusing on managers in the indoor sex industry. *Sexualities, 17*(5–6), 724–741. https://doi.org/10.1177/1363460714531271
Caelli, K., Ray, L., & Mill, J. (2003). 'Clear as mud': Towards greater clarity in generic qualitative research. *International Journal of Qualitative Methods, 2*(2), 1–13. https://doi.org/10.1177/160940690300200201
Canadian Homelessness Research Network (CHRN). (2013). *What works and for whom? A hierarchy of evidence for promising practices research*. Canadian Homelessness Research Network Press. Online: https://www.homelesshub.ca/sites/default/files/PPFramework_Part1.pdf
City of Port Phillip. (n.d.). Community grants program 2018-19: Successful recipients. Online: http://www.portphillip.vic.gov.au/default/SocialPlanningandPolicyDocuments/CoPP_Community%20Grants_2018%2019.pdf
Connelly, L., & Sanders, T. (2020). Disrupting the boundaries of the academe: Co-creating knowledge and sex work 'academic-activism'. In S. Walklate, K. FitzGibbon, J. McCulloch, & J. Maher (Eds.), *The Emerald handbook of feminism, criminology and social change* (pp. 203–218). Emerald.
Crowe, S., Cresswell, K., Robertson, A., Huby, G., Avery, A., & Sheikh, A. (2011). The case study approach. *BMC Medical Research Methodology, 27*(11), 100–109. https://doi.org/10.1186/1471-2288-11-100

Daley, K. (2015). The wrongs of protection: Balancing protection and participation in research with marginalised young people. *Journal of Sociology, 51*(2), 121–138. https://doi.org/10.1177/1440783313482365

de Vries, P. (2010). From slave to sex worker: Feminist debates on prostitution politics in The Netherlands, 1880-2000. *L'Homme, 21*(1), 29–47.

Doolin, B. (1998). Information technology and disciplinary technology: Being critical in interpretative research on information systems. *Journal of Information Technology, 13*, 301–311. https://doi.org/10.1177/026839629801300408

Fazal, N., Jackson, S., Wong, K., Yessis, J., & Jetha, N. (2017). Between worst and best: Developing criteria to identify promising practices in health promotion and disease prevention for the Canadian best practices portal. *Health Promotion and Chronic Disease Prevention in Canada: Research, Policy and Practice, 37*(11), 386–392. https://doi.org/10.24095/hpcdp.37.11.03

Gaynor, A., & Gifford, C. (2022). Sex workers: Citizenship status and identity, civic deficits, and exiting. *International Journal of Gender, Sexuality and Law, 2*, 252–272. https://www.northumbriajournals.co.uk/index.php/ijgsl/article/view/1262/1629

Giametta, C., & Le Bail, H. (2023). The national and moral borders of the 2016 French law on sex work: An analysis of the 'prostitution exit programme'. *Critical Social Policy, 43*(2), 214–233. https://doi.org/10.1177/02610183221101167

Gilmour, F. (2020). Careers in the Australian sex industry: Exploring life narratives through metaphor. *Journal of Sociology, 56*(3), 297–313. https://doi.org/10.1177/1440783319893462

Great Britain. (1871). *Report of the Royal Commission upon the administration and operation of the contagious diseases acts–Vol II.–minutes of evidence, &c.* Her Majesty's Stationery Office. https://wellcomecollection.org/works/nu5hxhbf

Green, J., & Thorogood, N. (2009). *Qualitative methods for health research.* Sage.

Gubrium, J., & Holstein, J. (2012). Narrative practice and the transformation of interview subjectivity. In J. Gubrium, J. Holstein, A. Marvasti, & K. McKinney (Eds.), *The SAGE handbook of interview research: The complexity of the craft* (Second ed., pp. 27–43). Sage.

Hanks, S. (2022). The safeguarding delusion: Sex work and policing in Wales. *Justice, Power and Resistance, 5*(1–2), 91–108. https://doi.org/10.1332/VYJF2519

Hesse-Biber, S. (2014). Feminist approaches to in-depth interviewing. In S. Hesse-Biber (Ed.), *Feminist research practice: A primer* (pp. 182–233). Sage.

Hollway, W., & Jefferson, T. (1997). Eliciting narrative through the in-depth interview. *Qualitative Inquiry, 3*(1), 53–70. https://doi.org/10.1177/107780049700300103

Jerrard, R. (1995). Prostitution: Defining terms. *Police Journal, 68*(2), 129–132.

Jovchelovitch, S., & Bauer, M. (2000). Narrative interviewing. In M. Bauer & G. Gaskell (Eds.), *Qualitative researching with text, image and sound* (pp. 57–74). Sage.

Karlsson, H. (2024). Reducing sex work by targeting 'vulnerable' sex workers: A post-structural analysis of policies regulating Danish exit programmes directed at people involved in sex work. *International Journal of Social Welfare, 33*(2), 446–456. https://doi.org/10.1111/ijsw.12611

Kempadoo, K. (2015). The modern-day white (wo)man's burden: Trends in anti-trafficking and anti-slavery campaigns. *Journal of Human Trafficking, 1*(1), 8–20. https://doi.org/10.1080/23322705.2015.1006120

Kennedy, K., Sandy, L., & Martinovic, M. (2023). Reentry support in Victoria, Australia: Managing risk, or fostering agency? *Journal of Offender Rehabilitation, 62*(1), 21–38. https://psycnet.apa.org/doi/10.1080/10509674.2022.2158984

Kofod, J. (2018). Business women and exit programs. *SAGE Open, 8*(4). https://doi.org/10.1177/2158244018809219

Law, T. (2013). Transitioning out of sex work: Exploring sex workers' experiences and perspectives. In E. van der Meulen, E. Durisin, & V. Love (Eds.), *Selling sex: Experience, advocacy, and research on sex work in Canada* (pp. 101–110). UBC Press.

Leigh, C. (1997). Inventing sex work. In J. Nagel (Ed.), *Whores and other feminists* (pp. 225–231). Routledge.

Levy, J., & Jakobsson, P. (2014). Sweden's abolitionist discourse and law: Effects on the dynamics of Swedish sex work and on the lives of Sweden's sex workers. *Criminology & Criminal Justice, 14*(5), 593–607. https://doi.org/10.1177/1748895814528926

Lincoln, Y., & Guba, E. (1985). *Naturalistic inquiry*. Sage.

Loomes, G. (2018). Researching about us without us: Exploring research participation and the politics of disability rights in the context of the Mental Capacity Act 2005. *Journal of Medical Ethics, 44*(6), 424–427. https://www.jstor.org/stable/26879752

Luna, F. (2009). Elucidating the concept of vulnerability: Layers not labels. *International Journal of Feminist Approaches to Bioethics, 2*(1), 121–139. https://doi.org/10.1111/dewb.12206

Månsson, S., & Hedin, U. (1999). Breaking the Matthew effect—On women leaving prostitution. *International Journal of Social Welfare, 8*, 67–77. https://doi.org/10.1111/1468-2397.00063

Mayhew, P., & Mossman, E. (2007). *Exiting prostitution: Models of best practice*. Crime and Justice Research Centre, Victoria University of Wellington. Online: https://www.nzpc.org.nz/pdfs/Mayhew-and-Mossman,-(2007c)-Exiting-Prostitution-Models-of-best-practice.pdf

Maynes, M., Pierce, J., & Laslett, B. (2012). *Telling stories: The use of personal narratives in the social sciences and history*. Cornell University Press.

McGinn, A. (2003). Prostitution, sexuality and the law in ancient Rome. Oxford.

Miles, M., & Huberman, M. (2019). *Qualitative data analysis: A methods sourcebook*. Sage.

Meek Lange, M., Rogers, W., & Dodds, S. (2013). Vulnerability in research ethics: A way forward. *Bioethics, 27*(6), 333–340. https://doi.org/10.1111/bioe.12032

Moniz, S., Karia, A., Khalid, A., & Vindrola-Padros, C. (2023). Stories for change: The impact of public narrative on the co-production process. *Health Expectations, 26*(2), 919–930. https://doi.org/10.1111/hex.13718

Neufeld, S., Chapman, J., Crier, N., Marsh, S., McLeod, J., & Deane, L. (2019). Research 101: A process for developing local guidelines for ethical research in heavily researched communities. *Harm Reduction Journal, 16*, 41–52. https://doi.org/10.1186/s12954-019-0315-5

Network of Sex Work Projects (NSWP). (2024). "Let's talk about sex work" - a terminology statement and guide. Online: https://www.nswp.org/resource/nswp-publications/lets-talk-about-sex-work-terminology-statement-and-guide

O'Neill, M., & Campbell, R. (2010). Desistance from sex work: Feminist cultural criminology and intersectionality—The complexities of moving in and out of sex work. In Y. Taylor, S. Hines, & M. Casey (Eds.), *Theorising intersectionality and sexuality* (pp. 163–189). Palgrave Macmillan.

Parliament of Victoria. (2017). 2017-18 budget estimates inquiry: Response to question taken on notice for the health portfolio at the consumer affairs, gaming and liquor regulations hearing held on 31 May 2017. Online: https://www.parliament.vic.gov.au/images/stories/committees/paec/2017-18_Budget_Estimates/QoNs_responses/Consumer_Affairs_Gaming__Liquor_Regulation_Question_2_response.pdf

Perkins, R. (1991). *Working girls: Prostitutes, their life and social control*. Australian Institute of Criminology.

Pitcher, J. (2015). Sex work and modes of self-employment in the informal economy: Diverse business practices and constraints to effective working. *Social Policy & Society, 14*(1), 113–123. https://doi.org/10.1017/S1474746414000426

Powell, A., & Sandy, L. (2015). *Promising practice in workplace and organisational approaches for the prevention of violence against women*. RMIT University.

Presser, L., & Sandberg, S. (2019). Narrative criminology as critical criminology. *Critical Criminology, 27*, 131–143. https://doi.org/10.1007/s10612-019-09437-9

Presser, L., & Sandberg, S. (2015). Introduction: What is the story? In L. Presser & S. Sandberg (Eds.), *Narrative criminology: Understanding stories of crime* (pp. 1–20). NYU Press.

Project Respect. (2008). *Evaluation of Project Respect's Pathways project*. Project Respect.

Resourcing Health and Education in the Sex Industry (RhED). (2013). *'Pathways to exit' program: Evaluation report, phase three, 1 March 2012–30 June 2013.* Unpublished report.

Rowlands, J. (2021). Interviewee transcript review as a tool to improve data quality and participant confidence in sensitive research. *International Journal of Qualitative Methods, 20*, 1–11. https://doi.org/10.1177/16094069211066170

Sanders, T., O'Neill, M., & Pitcher, J. (2009). *Prostitution: Sex work, policy and politics*. Sage.

Sandy, L. (2014). *Women and sex work in Cambodia: Blood, sweat and tears*. Routledge.

Sandy, L., Meenagh, J., & Nes-Iadicola, P. (2019a). *Transitioning programs for sex workers: Evidence review report*. RMIT University.

Sandy, L., Meenagh, J., & Nes-Iadicola, P. (2019b). *Transitioning programs for sex workers: An exploration of promising practice*. RMIT University.

Sawicki, D., Meffert, B., Read, K., & Heinz, A. (2019). Culturally competent health care for sex workers: An examination of myths that stigmatize sex work and hinder access to care. *Sexual and Relationship Therapy, 34*(3), 355–371. https://doi.org/10.1080/14681994.2019.1574970

Shareck, M., Buhariwala, P., Hassan, M., & O'Campo, P. (2020). Helping women transition out of sex work: Study protocol of a mixed-methods process and outcome evaluation of a sex work exiting program. *BMC Women's Health, 20*, 227–236. https://doi.org/10.1186/s12905-020-01086-3

Smith, A., & Pitts, M. (2007). Researching the margins: An introduction. In M. Pitts & A. Smith (Eds.), *Researching the margins: Strategies for ethical and rigorous research with marginalised communities* (pp. 3–41). Palgrave Macmillan.

State of Victoria. (2018). Community support fund operating statement 2017-18. Online: https://www.dtf.vic.gov.au/community-support-fund/community-support-fund-financial-overview-2017-18

Stella. (2013). Language matters: Talking about sex work. Online: https://www.nswp.org/sites/default/files/StellaInfoSheetLanguageMatters.pdf

Timmermans, M., Kuin, M., & van Leerdam, J. (2019). Summary evaluation of exit programmes for prostitutes scheme (RUPS II). Regioplan and Cebon. Online: https://repository.wodc.nl/bitstream/handle/20.500.12832/2413/2943a_summary_tcm28-384792.pdf

Joint United Nations Programme on HIV/AIDS (UNAIDS). (2012). *UNAIDS guidance note on HIV and sex work*. UNAIDS.

Varpio, L., Ajjawi, R., Monrouxe, L., O'Brien, B., & Rees, C. (2017). Shedding the cobra effect: Problematising thematic emergence, triangulation, saturation and member checking. *Medical Education, 51*(1), 40–50. https://doi.org/10.1111/medu.13124

Wahab, S. (2006). Evaluating the usefulness of a prostitution diversion project. *Qualitative Social Work, 5*, 67–92. https://doi.org/10.1177/1473325006061539

Walkowitz, J. (1982). *Prostitution and Victorian society: Women, class, and the state*. Cambridge University Press.

Yin, R. (2014). *Case study research, design and method*. Sage.

Legislation Cited

Sex Work Decriminalisation Act (Victoria) (2022).

Street Offences Act (England) (1959).

Vagrancy Act (England) (1824).

CHAPTER 2

Exiting Assumptions: The Shaping and Framing of 'Exiting' Programs

Abstract 'Exiting' programs set out to help sex workers leave the sex industry and are usually accompanied by an attempt to 'reform' and 'rehabilitate' sex workers. In this chapter, we explore how sex work is conceptualised in these programs, and start this by unpacking the conceptual framings to highlight some of the underlying assumptions in 'exiting' studies. We do this to show how sex work is framed as a dangerous and harmful activity that people are either trapped in, escaping, or have survived. When sex work is framed this way there is an assumption that workers want to leave the industry because doing sex work is seen as traumatising. While this may be the case for some people, it is not an experience shared by all sex workers, and we show the problems with this assumption and the narrow understanding of 'exiting' it encourages. Ultimately, we argue for a need to reconsider the one-dimensional views of sex work shaping 'exiting' frameworks and for research and theories to move beyond viewing 'exiting' through a lens of addiction and recovery, and sex work as something someone is either 'in' or 'out' of.

Keywords Sex work, Exiting models, Violence against women, Deviance, Rehabilitation, Stigma, Morality politics, Theory

L. Sandy et al., *Reconceptualizing Exiting and Career Development in Sex Work*, Palgrave Advances in Sex Work Studies,
https://doi.org/10.1007/978-3-032-10077-1_2

2.1 Introduction

In 'exiting' studies, the major theoretical framings shaping understandings and interventions have developed from understanding sex work as a violation of human rights and a form of violence against women and girls (VAWG). In this chapter, we provide an overview of the four key models developed to explain 'exiting', and in doing this, we have two aims: a) to outline the current ideology behind 'exiting' sex work and b) critique the support for, and rise of, 'exiting' programs globally, particularly under VAWG or anti-trafficking prevention efforts. We criticise the attempt to 'reform' and 'rehabilitate' sex workers through 'exiting' programs on account of how sex work is reduced to a monolithic explanation of a form of violence against women, which allows us to highlight the damaging effects of current policy and ideology, while showing how sex workers are rarely outside of a system of power and inequality (Bowen, 2021; Sandy, 2014). The conceptual framing and underlying assumptions behind 'exiting' are examined through the lens of sex work as work, and here we illuminate how the underlying desire to eradicate sex work informing these approaches perpetuates the stigmatisation and marginalisation of sex workers as 'others'. Throughout our examination of the discourses and theoretical framings surrounding 'exiting', we argue that the governance of sex work via 'exiting' results in research frameworks, policies and programs that operate from an understanding of sex work as harm. This produces interventions that incorporate contradictory messages and practices and pathologises sex workers, ultimately excluding them from inclusion because of the 'vulnerable' status accorded to them in 'exiting' frameworks.

We start the chapter by problematising how the exit process has been theorised. Most 'exiting' research has focused on street sex work, which means most sex workers are largely ignored in these studies. We examine the 'breakaway model' as this is the foundational model for 'exiting' research. This model was developed in Sweden by Månsson and Hedin, who used role-exit theory to explain how women stopped sex working. Role-exit theory centres on how people breakaway from addictions like alcohol or drug consumption, and as the chapter moves through other models, we highlight the issues surrounding sex work characterised by pathology and denial of agency. In the breakaway model, sex workers are said to be 'integrated in the milieu', an idea paralleled in the following model we explore called the 'integrated model'. This model extends on

Månsson and Hedin's earlier work by incorporating 'stages of change' theory, and in our discussion, we highlight the issues with using frameworks drawn from the field of addiction studies. We do this to show how these major theoretical framings have developed from an understanding of sex work as a social disease or problem, and sex workers as engaging in 'self-destructive' behaviour, which we argue, perpetuates pathologising and victimising sex workers as a category. We end this chapter by exploring alternative framings developed through grounded research with diverse sex workers that aimed to document their routine pathways out of sex work. These typologies ask us to think differently about sex work and 'exiting' by considering 'exiting' experiences as part of working patterns and career trajectories. These typologies also allow us to challenge 'role-exit' and 'stages of change' framings as being inadequate conceptual tools to understand sex workers' experiences and working practices. We conclude the chapter by arguing for the need to reconceptualise 'exiting' as career development and using practice theory to develop more grounded theories based on workers' lived experiences.

2.2 "Leaving a Life": Framing Role-Exits

Fuchs Ebaugh's (1988) model of 'role-exit' is arguably one of the most influential models in the development of 'exiting' programs. At a superficial level, role-exit theory may seem a good fit with 'exiting', but there are some issues with the models that have developed from this theoretical perspective. Fuchs Ebaugh's work explores the key stages people go through as they leave a role: first doubts; seeking alternatives and weighing these up; turning points and how they function in the role-exit process; and establishing an ex-role identity (Fuchs Ebaugh, 1988, see also Månsson & Hedin, 1999; Oselin, 2010). Fuchs Ebaugh argues that, while some people may go through role-exit in a linear way, this will not be the case for all, as others may return to previous roles, and there is no predetermined amount of time for a person to move through each stage as a role-exit depends on a person's individual and social circumstances (Ouspenski, 2014).

2.2.1 Breaking the 'Matthew Effect': The Breakaway Model

Fuchs Ebaugh's work on role-exit is quite popular and as a result many 'exiting' models have been influenced by this, including Månsson and

Hedin's breakaway model—a model that has played a very central role in conceptualisations of 'exiting'. Månsson and Hedin's model was based on a study with twenty-three Swedish female sex workers (15 had left the industry, 8 were still working). Most of their participants were street-based workers and about a third worked indoors. Their model consists of five stages: drifting into sex work; ensnarement in sex work; pre-breakaway; breakaway; and after the breakaway or stabilisation—a sixth stage may include re-entry (Månsson & Hedin, 1999, p. 67). In further developing the concept of 'role-exit' in sex work, Hedin and Månsson (2004, p. 225) went on to propose a theory for understanding how women "breakaway from prostitution", identifying four phases of breakaway, which they describe as:

(1). *Preliminary stages of the breakaway*, when the woman is thinking about quitting, seeking alternatives to the sex trade and trying various strategies in order to distance herself from prostitution and to locate the resources and points of support needed for another life.

(2). *The turning-point*, when the woman is in the process of deciding to actually break away. This can happen quickly and dramatically, or it can be a more gradual process.

(3). *The post-breakaway marginal situation*, when the woman finds herself dangling between two life patterns, living in a state of uncertainty and ambivalence. Here she encounters a number of challenges.

(4). *Building a new life*, when the women [sic] develop new roles through work, studies or parenthood. Gradually, old injuries are repaired, and a new life develops (Hedin & Månsson, 2004, p. 225).

Their model conceptualises sex work is lived, and experienced as purely harmful, as shown in the following claim:

> As we know it, the women's ability to escape an unbearable reality through fantasy plays a major role during their time in prostitution. Moreover, the ability to dream and fantasize is also important after the breakaway. A natural comparison might be between prostitutes' experiences and those who have been captured or locked up in, for example, prisons or concentration camps. Being able to imagine another life and to think differently

about how this life can become a reality can be a crucial survival strategy (Månsson & Hedin, 1999, p. 74).

Here we can see how these psycho-analytical descriptions and the monolithic explanation of sex work as violence against women led Månsson and Hedin to make some rather remarkable comparisons between sex workers and holocaust survivors.

In Månsson and Hedin's work, it is the turning points that lead to a sex worker's decision to leave the industry. Although they argue that structural, relational and individual factors influence a woman's decision to leave, ultimately a worker's emotional commitment becomes the determining factor in this model (Koostra, 2010, p. 11). Here we can see how Månsson and Hedin's interpretation was influenced by highly individualised models of personal choice and Merton's sociological concept of the 'Matthew Effect'. In addition to the breakaway model being heavily influenced by Fuchs Ebaugh's role-exit theory, Månsson and Hedin drew on Vanwesenbeeck's (1994) study of well-being and risk for sex workers in the Netherlands. In her study, Vanwesenbeeck set out to challenge "scientific theory and research [that] sees prostitution a priori as a form of deviant behavior and searches for associations with unhealthiness, sickness, pathology, and the distortion of 'normal' human existence" (1994, p. 39). In *Prostitutes' Well-Being and Risk*, Vanwesenbeeck aimed to "prove these wrong" by creating a coherent, more representative picture of sex workers' well-being with a large and diverse sample. When discussing differences in well-being and risk management, Vanwesenbeeck employed Merton's idea of the Matthew Effect, which she saw as useful for explaining how "sociological and psychological phenomena reinforce each other mutually" (1994, p. 154). Vanwesenbeeck interpreted the Matthew Effect as "the result of an either fortunate or fatal interaction between an individual and his or her surroundings" and used Merton's idea to explain how people who experienced childhood sexual abuse and trauma may expose themselves to increased risk in adulthood (1994, p. 154). In sex work, Vanwesenbeeck argued this may result in workers not using condoms and accepting client abuse and mistreatment, which then reinforces low self-esteem (1994, p. 153–6). Conversely, Vanwesenbeeck used this concept to also explore how workers had enjoyable careers in sex work and reported high levels of job satisfaction and professional attitudes (1994, p. 153–6). Her work explored the interaction between internal and external factors in women's lives, leading

Månsson and Hedin to describe this as the 'interplay model', which they set out to integrate with Fuchs Ebaugh's role-exit theory.

In most sociological studies, the Matthew Effect is about the rich-poor dichotomy and is used to explain how those who have power and status are often placed in situations where they gain more power and status (essentially, advantage begets advantage). On the other hand, those who do not have power and status will struggle to improve their lot. In Månsson and Hedin's work, however, they attach solely negative consequences to sex work, leading them to discredit sex workers' desires to be recognised as professional workers recorded by Vanwesenbeeck. In their study, Månsson and Hedin use this sociological concept to refer to cumulative disadvantage and a feedback loop where the more unstable the environment is, the less likely people will think about their future and behaviour becomes less forwarding looking. While this may encourage analysis of structural factors, the model presents a lopsided picture with sex workers presented as being in a pathological state of helplessness and as miserable, neurotic, or self-destructive. Moreover, it is 'reckless' behaviour by some that is said to create a 'chaotic environment' which encourages similar behaviour by others. Here, the idea of the Matthew Effect is reversed, with disadvantage begetting disadvantage and, as Rigney notes, for the women in Månsson and Hedin's research, attempting to break the downward cycle is "a painful and precarious process" (2010, p. 58).

In their breakaway model, Månsson and Hedin "put individual responsibility of the sex worker or 'responsibilization' to the front" (Koostra, 2010, p. 11). This responsibilisation leads to the denial of sex workers' agency and sees them as victims of exploitation and chaotic environments (Koostra, 2010; Ouspenski, 2014). Sanders (2007) has also criticised the breakaway model for its failure to consider the interplay between individual agency and structural factors, including factors like the lack of appropriate and safe and secure housing, lack of drug treatment programs (and relative ineffectiveness of some programs), lack of realistic and appropriate vocational training and alternative employment as well as sex work criminalisation. For Sanders (2007), putting all the focus on sex workers emphasises victimisation and does little to address the structural barriers that can make it difficult to leave.

The model has some problematic elements as the language used pathologises sex work and sex workers. It adopts a deficits-based approach that focuses on understanding women's involvement in sex work as an accumulation of negative experiences and deprivation. For example, Månsson and Hedin describe a range of factors contributing to women's involvement in sex work, but this is seen in exclusively negative terms:

> ...the way into the sex trade constitutes the culmination of a long chain of previous, destructive events ... a cycle of victimization characterized by insufficient emotional connection, sexual abuse, sexual exploitation during the teenage years, rape experiences and, later on, prostitution. Central to the process is the incorporation of inadequate self-esteem ... many of the women were labelled as "whores" early, often long before their actual entry into prostitution (Månsson & Hedin, 1999, p. 71).

This leads to a one-dimensional view of sex workers as victims, and sees sex working women purely as damaged, supporting the conclusion that sex work, as damaging and harmful, is something women need to escape. We can see this with sex work being described as something women are 'trapped' in and sex workers living 'chaotic lives' reflected in the model's rhetoric of women being "ensnared" in sex work and needing to "breakaway" and "stabilise" (Månsson & Hedin, 1999, p. 74). The focus then becomes transforming irresponsible, chaotic and damaged women into responsible, self-managing people, with programs then targeting individual behaviours and thinking patterns and downplaying factors connected to social considerations and disadvantage. Consequently, 'exiting' programs designed to support sex working women to stop selling sex are argued to be the logical mechanism through which to reduce the harms associated with sex work and sex worker rehabilitation is seen as an unproblematic strategy, even when this is forced (as we need to save sex workers from themselves).

Månsson and Hedin's research, and the breakaway model, was part of feminist lobbying for female sex workers to be understood as victims of violence and the adoption of welfare-based 'desistance' models designed to stop people from buying and selling sex. At the time of Månsson and Hedin's study, the Swedish Parliament passed legislation that criminalised buying sexual services (client criminalisation). What we can see in Månsson and Hedin's breakaway model is a form of 'enforced welfarism', in which, as Scoular and O'Neill (2007) argue, a woman's identity becomes fixed as the 'prostitute-victim'. In this framing, sex workers are "responsibilised to exit sex work, with limited agency or voice, excluded from certain forms of citizenship, and whose only socially acceptable 'moral' option is to exit sex work or be labelled as deviant or criminal" (O'Neill & Jobe, 2022, p. 69). Thus, we can see how this model is connected to moral engineering efforts linked with the governance of sex work through 'exiting', and this is a pattern replicated in other 'exiting' frameworks.

2.3 Changing "Self-Destructive" Behaviour: Stages of Change Theories and Role-Exits

Stages of change is another highly influential behaviour change model adapted to explain leaving sex work. Based on the stages of change model developed by Prochaska, DiClemente and Norcross (1992), later-generation integrated 'exiting' models built on role-exit theory by focusing on the six stages of change identified in this model. This includes pre-contemplation (person does not see an issue with what they are doing); contemplation (ambivalent state); decision (person makes a decision and is getting ready for change); action (person makes the change); maintenance (changes have been fully integrated in the person's life); and lapse/relapse (return to old behaviour) (Prochaska et al., 1992). While this behaviour change model is useful in identifying a person's readiness for change, the model was originally developed to describe the process people go through when quitting smoking, which continues in the legacy of viewing leaving sex work through a lens of addiction and recovery. The model itself was developed to theorise the process of changing what are destructive behavioural patterns and creating new patterns free of "problematic behaviours" (Prochaska et al., 1992, p. 1103). In this section we look at the model developed by Baker et al. (2010) using stages of change theory to explain the process of leaving sex work.

2.3.1 Reaching "Final Exit": The Integrated Model

Baker, Dalla and Williamson developed this model for "exiting prostitution" based on a review of existing models and their work with street-based "prostituted women" in the US and the stages of change model (2010, p. 579). Baker, Dalla and Williamson's integrated model highlights six key stages:

1. Immersion: "the starting point wherein a woman is totally immersed in prostitution and has no thoughts of leaving or any conscious awareness of the need to change" (Baker et al., 2010, p. 590).
2. Awareness: at this stage, a worker becomes aware of the need to change, but may start to recognise the barriers that prevent leaving, and the stage is comprised of two parts:
   a. Visceral awareness: where "a woman experiences 'gut' feelings about leaving prostitution, yet these feelings cannot be (or are not) articulated to herself or to others" (Baker et al., 2010, p. 591); and
   b. Conscious awareness: whereby a woman "acknowledges her feelings and begins to process them consciously thereby enabling her to verbalize what she had previously felt at the gut level" (Baker et al., 2010, p. 591).
3. Deliberate Planning: where "a woman begins assessing both formal and informal support resources" and may begin making contact with formal support providers (Baker et al., 2010, p. 592).
4. Initial Exit: "when the woman begins actively using informal (e.g., moving in with a family member) and formal (e.g., attending counseling, entering de-tox) support services" but her "internal desire and motivation to exit are severely tested" which may prevent her from leaving (Baker et al., 2010, p. 592).
5. Re-entry: where a worker may cycle through all or some of the stages again before achieving final exit.
6. Final Exit: where a worker leaves the sex industry, permanently or for some period of time before re-entering.

In their integrated model, Baker, Dalla and Williamson identify barriers preventing people leaving sex work and differentiate between the individual, relational, structural and societal factors shaping this. Individual level barriers are associated with women's own internal drives and abilities and include "self-destructive" behaviour, substance use, mental health problems and lack of knowledge about services available (Baker et al., 2010, p. 588). Relational level barriers are close relationships and social networks and include factors like strained family relations, social isolation, facilitators, or other third parties and drug dealers who they see as keeping workers in the sector (Baker et al., 2010). Structural barriers are societal circumstances that include limited job skills and employment opportunities, lack of appropriate and safe housing, lack of economic self-sufficiency and inadequate services, and at the societal level, stigma and discrimination (Baker et al., 2010). Their model acknowledges that people may go back to sex working, and how some people can cycle through the stages of change several times until they reach the 'final exit'.

Although the integrated model does attempt to account for individual and structural factors, the analysis ends up highlighting deficits in sex workers by focusing only on the individual factors that challenge a worker's exit (e.g., no coping skills, lack of confidence and initiative). This means that, while the model may purport to consider structural and societal factors, ultimately, it remains focused on individualised understandings and is unable to account for women's sex work careers and how these are shaped by gendered employment practices, gendered social roles and friendship networks in sex work settings (Gilmour, 2020; Maher et al., 2013). When discussing women re-entering sex work, Baker, Dalla and Williamson claim that at this stage, sex workers' behaviour can be challenging for support organisations because "their lack of behavioral action makes them invisible to support providers" (2010, p. 593). As Bowen argues, this framing is problematic, as at the crux of this claim is "researchers suggesting that sex workers need to be more accommodating to support organizations instead of the opposite being true", and what it also shows is how the responsibilising of sex workers becomes central in these frameworks (2015, p. 433).

A central feature of this model is helping workers acknowledge the negative effects of sex work, so women can recognise the harms and leave sex work. This is made clear in their discussion of the 'immersion' and 'awareness' stages. Being 'immersed' in sex work suggests women lack self-awareness and are unable to see the harm they are doing to themselves, or the need for behavioural change: "a woman is totally immersed in prostitution and has no thoughts of leaving or any conscious awareness of the need to change" (Baker et al., 2010, p. 590). Awareness may come through "gut feelings about leaving prostitution", and it here that they elide sex worker agency and decision-making abilities by claiming that some workers deny this awareness, while others lack this ability or awareness and will never move beyond immersion (Baker et al., 2010, p. 591). Here the claim is that sex workers are almost infantile, existing in a pre-contemplative state where they are unable to see an issue with their behaviour and cannot recognise the damage they are doing to themselves. Like the breakaway model, this works to justify the need for 'exiting' programs and rescue-based approaches, underpinned by the logic of saving sex workers mostly from themselves. The lack of worker agency is also reflected in their use of the term 'prostituted women', which denies sex worker agency, and their capacity to act, think and decide for themselves, instead casting sex workers as objects of exploitation (NSWP, 2024, p. 6). This is a gendered term that suggests ‘prostitution’ is done to sex workers (chiefly women), and many sex workers consider this language “disrespectful, alienating and as invisiblizing their realities” (Stella, 2013, p. 3).

In setting out to explain the “barriers to prostitution exit”, Baker, Dalla and Williamson construct sex work as something women are trapped in (2010, p. 587). The logical conclusion drawn from the integrated model is that sex work is harmful, and women need help to leave, whether they know it or not. While the model includes individual and structural factors, it overwhelmingly fails to consider the agentic capacities and socially situated identities of workers and how professional identities shape sex workers’ work practices and experiences (Bilardi et al., 2011; Gilmour, 2016; Maher et al., 2013; Vanwesenbeeck, 2017). The integrated model mentions the “shame and stigma of prostitution” as part of the “complex web of factors” inhibiting ‘exit’ but does little to understand and address the impacts of stigma and how sex workers social status and control over working conditions are impacted by this (Baker et al., 2010, p. 583). It also fails to consider negative social reactions to doing sex work, as sex workers’ emotional health is shaped by stigma, which includes being discriminated against, facing difficulties in combining work and private life and the fear of being found out (Platt et al., 2018; Vanwesenbeeck, 2017). Bowen (2015) and Sanders (2007) address some of these criticisms in their conceptual models, which we explore in the following section; however, their models are more typologies than theoretical frameworks and while they are useful in describing practices and classifying experiences, they face limitations because of this, but do suggest a way forward in reconceptualising ‘exiting’.

2.4 Typologies of ‘Exiting’

The next two models we consider are more like classification systems or typologies that offer an understanding of leaving sex work based on key characteristics and themes identified in research with sex workers. We have included these two models as they add to our discussion of how ‘exiting’ has been conceptualised in research and, as they have come from sex workers’ direct experiences, offer a more grounded understanding of the phenomenon.

2.4.1 *Typology of Transitions*

Sanders' (2007, p. 81-90) typology of transitions was based on a study with thirty UK-based female sex workers (15 ex-outdoor workers and 15 ex-indoor workers). The work offers an alternative perspective to the theories discussed above as Sanders attempted to develop a typology of transitions out of sex work for both indoor and outdoor workers, rather than treating sex workers as a homogenous group. In her study, Sanders identified four types of transitioning, or routine pathways out of sex work, and specific triggers for indoor and outdoor workers according to each transition type, which we have summarised in Table 2.1.

Sanders' model addresses the main reasons for workers leaving sex work, which is important in understanding motivations and desires. The 'triggers' can also help in understanding events that could lead to workers wanting to leave sex work, and the type of transitioning she identified in the research. For example, in the 'reactionary' category, Sanders discussed how the reasons for leaving sex work were often in direct response to significant life events, and this meant that the reasons, and hence the desire to leave sex work, may not be as permanent as the other types of transitions she identified in the model. On the other hand, in the 'gradual planning' category, Sanders suggests that workers often had a focused plan on leaving sex work, with some using agencies to access

Table 2.1 Typology of transitions

Type of transition	*Trigger for street worker*	*Trigger for indoor worker*
Reactionary	Violence, ill health, significant life events (e.g., pregnancy/ child removal, imprisonment)	New relationship, being discovered, violence
Gradual planning	Drug treatment program, rehousing, welfare support, therapeutic engagement	Timed transition alongside alternative career and financial planning
Natural progression	Desire for a new, safer lifestyle that is drug free, concerned about working conditions	Age, natural career length, disillusionment with working conditions/lack of regulation
Yo-yoing	Failed drug treatment and support package, drift in and out, criminal justice involvement	Unplanned exit, psychological strain, working 'on and off'/career break

Source Sanders, 2007, p. 81.

services, including drug and alcohol treatment. In this type of transition, a worker may also limit the amount of time they are engaged in sex work or the number of clients they see. This process takes longer and was a more prepared one, with the workers who used this strategy saving money to prepare for a reduction in income (more common among indoor workers), while outdoor workers tended to reduce the number of clients or started drug therapy. 'Natural progression', akin to retirement, accounted for the experiences of workers closer to retirement age (i.e., getting older and receiving less clients or being fed up with working conditions as factors for indoor workers wanting to leave), while for outdoor workers this may be wanting a lifestyle free of drug use and the fear of violence or actual violence.

The 'yo-yoing' pattern of moving in and out of sex work held for indoor and outdoor workers. Many workers in Sanders' study were in this category, and as Ouspenski (2014) suggests this may be because they lacked a strong and workable plan for leaving sex work. It also indicates the difficulties some workers face when trying to leave, which are factors also explored by Baker, Dalla and Williamson in their integrated model (2010). Here Sanders (2007) suggests that workers may come back because of financial reasons or starting to use drugs again and the need for money. To explain worker perceptions in this category, indoor workers told Sanders that sometimes they needed 'time out', leading Sanders to argue that the lack of good working conditions causes significant occupational stress and strain as sex workers do not receive sick leave or paid holidays, and highly regulated working conditions and exploitative management practices means bosses expect people to work long shifts and frequent days (Sanders, 2007, p. 88). Further, indoor workers 'yo-yoed' because the money they earned in 'normal' jobs in mainstream labour markets was inadequate compared with the income earned in sex work. In these cases, 'yo-yoing' was often accompanied by an unplanned 'exit'. For outdoor workers, involvement with criminal justice agencies often set 'yo-yoing' in motion, with some workers returning to sex work to pay fines, while other workers without planned transitions moved back into sex work because of the need to earn money for drugs (Sanders, 2007, p. 87).

Sanders' model considers the gendered and socioeconomic constraints workers face, and adopting a rights-based approach allowed her to consider sex workers' individual agency without downplaying the barriers faced in leaving sex work. For some workers, leaving sex work was not something that happened quickly, and it was a long process that was not straightforward. Unlike the other models discussed above, Sanders' study "withholds a moral condemnation of sex work" and "provides pragmatic tools on how to assist sex workers best if they choose to leave sex work" (Koostra, 2010, p. 13). However, as Bowen (2015, p. 433) highlights, the key issue with this model is the focus on leaving sex work, and as a result re-entry is depicted as chaotic (i.e., 'yo-yoing'), which is similar to the framing of re-entry in the breakaway and integrated models discussed earlier. Here we argue that this framing is a consequence of the binary in/out categorisation influencing these theoretical frameworks.

2.4.2 *Sex-Work-no-More, Sex-Work-Maybe, Dual-Life*

Bowen's (2015) duality model is based on a study with twenty-two active and former off-street sex workers from Vancouver (18 women, 3 men and 1 gender queer worker). In her study, 17 participants had left sex work, and five were sex working at the time of interview. This model offers a different perspective on 'exiting' as, unlike the other studies, it focuses on the experiences of indoor workers. In her research, Bowen identified three different types of transitioning statuses: sex-work-no-more; sex-work-maybe; and dual-life, each of which we explain below.

Among former workers, Bowen (2015) identified nine as part of a 'sex-work-no-more' category. In this category, some of the reasons for leaving sex work included being in love or falling out of love, health conditions, or frustration with sex work. For those in the sex-work-no-more category, "leaving the industry was a way to eliminate harm, gain control over their lives, and align thoughts about sex work with their behaviors" (Bowen, 2015, p. 438). Bowen (2015) identified eight participants as fitting the sex-work-maybe category. Their reasons for leaving sex work were like those in the sex-work-no-more category, and some were hesitant about returning to sex work because of having a stable 'square' (non-sex work) job or being in love, and uncertainty about how engaging in sex work may affect sobriety and mental health. Other workers in this category spoke about concerns with contemporary sex work practices and maintaining personal boundaries (e.g., the rising popularity of the girlfriend experience). The participants in this category viewed sex work as an option for future employment, with some explaining how their "relationship with sex work felt unfinished: 'I don't think that I'm done with [sex work] … I would go back … I would ideally do it in a more intentional way'"

(Bowen, 2015, p. 439). The dual-life category accounted for a large part of Bowen's sample (15 participants). Dual-life sex workers worked simultaneously in sex work and 'square' work. This, Bowen (2015, p. 444) claims, challenges conventional thinking as the 'dual-life' category exemplifies the many ways people do sex work. For some workers, the dual-life category reduced burnout and frustration and saw them find a balance between working just enough in sex work to get the income needed, and not so much that it caused burnout or frustration (Bowen, 2015, p. 440).

Bowen's (2015) model raises a few critical points for discussion. First, in the three categories, sex workers' meaning making of their careers, and how the engaged in sex work, challenges conventional understandings of workers as needing 'saving' or sex work as purely harm. The idea of a worker's relationship with sex work feeling "unfinished" or wanting to do sex work in "a more intentional way" confounds mainstream ideas about 're-entry' as relapse, a negative term often associated with addiction, or as chaotic or disorderly with the idea of yo-yoing, as related to structural factors. In most studies, re-entry was framed as being 'trapped' in sex work and read as a person's failure to break away from the 'milieu' and thrive in 'conventional' work (see, for example, Baker et al., 2010; Hedin & Månsson, 2004; Mayhew & Mossman, 2007; Sanders, 2007). It also challenges the idea of 'sex work as a last resort', which often frames 'exiting' research, as reflected in Månsson and Hedin's work:

> The concept of resilience is used to describe children who, even when they are growing up in circumstances of poverty, exploitation and oppression, manage to develop a means to survive, display good intellectual capacities and have an ability to avoid or overcome sorrow or disappointment ... The term *dandelion children* is sometimes used to label these children. However, it can be argued that this expression is hardly relevant where the women in our study are concerned. They probably would not have ended up in prostitution had they been "super-kids" (1999, p. 75).

The understanding of sex work as work allows Bowen (2015) to argue that some people re-start sex work because they want to, and 'sex-work-maybe' was a way to keep their options open. With the idea of sex-work-maybe, workers can control how and when they 'exit', and instead of this being chaotic, Bowen's work shows how some workers are demonstrating and exercising agency in setting their own agenda and timeline and leaving (or not leaving) sex work in their own way. For the dual-life group, sex work allowed them to get additional income and was the best way for them to do sex work, for others it allowed them to address precarious working conditions in the sex industry like limited benefits (Sanders, 2007). For example, Theresa told Bowen: "I want to have medical plan, sick leave, vacation pay … I want that option in my life" (Bowen, 2015, p. 444). The dual-life category allowed Theresa to access employment benefits and conditions not available in sex work, while the flexible working arrangements in sex work supported this duality. Stigma and discrimination were a key concern for this group, as one of the most pressing issues they faced was the need to manage information to avoid discrimination (Bowen, 2015, p. 444). Clearly, keeping options open gives some workers a sense of economic security, and as Bowen suggests, there is a "need for openness and candor around reentry in the conceptualization of transition programs. Sex workers need space to explore reentry and position them[selves] in relation to it" (2015, p. 440).

Bowen's study shows the importance of thinking differently about sex work and 'exiting'—and more specifically, of how we can begin reconfiguring this through the prism of career planning and development. Her model pushes us to consider 'exiting' experiences as part of working patterns and as playing a key role in sex workers' working lives and career trajectories, of meaning making in their careers and experiences in sex work. Unlike the other major models surveyed in this chapter, it allows us to consider leaving sex work and clearly locate this within the fabric of workers' actual lives. In her model, we can recognise the broader socioeconomic forces shaping workers' lives and choices, forces that are often downplayed or ignored in the in/out binary that dominates the major theoretical frameworks, and in turn policy and discourse about sex work.

2.5 Conclusion

In this chapter, we surveyed the four main models conceptualising sex work 'exiting'. Our analyses have shown that most studies are based on the experiences of street-based cis women, even though in many countries, street sex work is the least prevalent form of sex work (Harcourt & Donovan, 2005). Street sex work has the largest number of workers who do want to leave, and research shows that workers in this sector experience higher levels of violence and abuse (Deering et al., 2014; Platt et al., 2018). However, the continued focus on street-based sex working women in ‘exiting’ research means that a broader understanding of ‘exiting’ has not developed. Sanders (2007) and Bowen (2015) clearly demonstrate the need for more diversity in research as their work highlights some significant differences in how workers make sense of the practice in their everyday lives. This is a significant issue as not all sex workers want to leave sex work, and for the workers who do not want to leave, many find themselves working in situations where they do not have the same labour rights and protections as other workers (Gaynor & Gifford, 2022; Weinhold, 2022). It also means that a broader understanding of practices in terms of careers in the sex industry is non-existent. Further research on the career trajectories and ‘exiting’ experiences of online, migrant, racialised, trans, male, gender diverse and queer sex workers would make valuable contributions to research.

In this chapter, we have unpacked the small number of studies that have developed formal conceptual frameworks to explain sex work ‘exiting’. Through this, we have shown how role-exit and stages of change theories are inadequate (and inappropriate) conceptual tools, largely because of their inability to account for culture, agency and marginalisation, other than through a lens of deviancy. This may be due to the frameworks themselves being located within functionalist social psychology, and so while they can provide us with a descriptive framework, they fall short in accounting for structural factors and cultural dimensions, and the larger web of relations sex work and sex workers are a part of (Wacquant, 1990). Other frameworks like Sanders’ typologies of transitions and Bowen’s duality model offer more insight into how people interact with social structures and the influence of social positioning in determining a person’s access to resources and power, rights and social obligations. This suggests that practice theory could offer some insight into how people’s actions within specific social positions are shaped by the structures and norms of that position, but, as Bowen (2021) signals, we need a bit more work here to understand the broader social contexts in which people are positioned and how their actions are enabled and constrained by social positions and shaped by intersecting structures like race, gender, age, sexuality, abilities and so on.

Although there is a growing body of research documenting the range of sexualities, relationships, practices and experiences in sex work and diversity in social settings were sex is sold, from public to private and online spaces, ‘exiting’ research and frameworks remain largely focused on cis women selling sex in heterosexual exchanges (Easterbrook-Smith,

2022; Laing et al., 2015; Matthews, 2024; Sanders et al., 2016; Sandy, 2014; Su & Valiquette, 2022). This area of work maintains the historical focus on public (on street) female sex work, which continues to dominate thinking and shape current understandings of sex work and sex workers as deviants (O'Neill & Jobe, 2022). In this chapter, we have shown how 'exiting' research frameworks have approached sex work based on a gendered understanding as purely harm. In the following chapter, we explore the consequences of this framing in policy interventions that pathologise and exclude sex workers, who are deemed vulnerable or in need of protection, and as Bowen argues this often results in "ineffectual strategies, limited in their applicability and lacking in material benefit to sex workers" (2015, p. 437). We have shown how we need to reconsider the one-dimensional views of sex work in research and policy if we are to develop theories that can account for sex workers diverse experiences and understanding sex work as work presents a way pathway towards this.

References

Baker, L., Dalla, R., & Williamson, C. (2010). Exiting prostitution: An integrated model. *Violence Against Women, 16*(5), 579–600. https://doi.org/10.1177/1077801210367643

Bilardi, J., Miller, A., Hocking, J., Keogh, L., Cummings, R., Chen, M., Bradshaw, C., & Fairley, C. (2011). The job satisfaction of female sex workers working in licensed brothels in Victoria, Australia. *The Journal of Sexual Medicine, 8*(1), 116–122. https://doi.org/10.1111/j.1743-6109.2010.01967.x

Bowen, R. (2021). *Work, money and duality: Trading sex as a side hustle*. Bristol University Press.

Bowen, R. (2015). Squaring up: Experiences of transition from off-street sex work to square work and duality—Concurrent involvement in both—in Vancouver, BC. *Canadian Review of Sociology, 52*(4), 429–449. https://doi.org/10.1111/cars.12085

Deering, K., Amin, A., Shoveller, J., Nesbitt, A., Garcia-Moreno, C., Duff, P., et al. (2014). A systematic review of the correlates of violence against sex workers. *American Journal of Public Health, 104*(5), e42–e54.

Easterbrook-Smith, G. (2022). OnlyFans as gig-economy work: A nexus of precarity and stigma. *Porn Studies, 10*(3), 252–267. https://doi.org/10.1080/23268743.2022.2096682

Fuchs Ebaugh, H. (1988). *Becoming an ex: The process of role exit*. University of Chicago Press.

Gaynor, A., & Gifford, C. (2022). Sex workers: Citizenship status and identity, civic deficits, and exiting. *International Journal of Gender, Sexuality and Law, 2*, 252–272. https://www.northumbriajournals.co.uk/index.php/ijgsl/article/view/1262/1629

Gilmour, F. (2020). Careers in the Australian sex industry: Exploring life narratives through metaphor. *Journal of Sociology, 56*(3), 297–313. https://doi.org/10.1177/1440783319893462

Gilmour, F. (2016). Work conditions and job mobility in the Australian indoor sex industry. *Sociological Research Online, 21*(4), 147–158. https://doi.org/10.5153/sro.4166

Harcourt, C., & Donovan, B. (2005). The many faces of sex work. *Sexually Transmitted Infections, 81*, 201–206. https://doi.org/10.1136/sti.2004.012468

Hedin, U., & Månsson, S. (2004). The importance of supportive relationships among women leaving prostitution. *Journal of Trauma Practice, 2*(3–4), 223–237. https://doi.org/10.1300/J189v02n03_13

Koostra, T. (2010). *Move forward! First results of the move forward project on career opportunities for sex workers*. Ministry of Foreign Affairs of the Netherlands.

Laing, M., Pilcher, K., & Smith, N. (Eds.). (2015). *Queer sex work*. Routledge.

Maher, J., Pickering, S., & Gerard, A. (2013). *Sex work: Labour, mobility, and sexual services*. Routledge.

Månsson, S., & Hedin, U. (1999). Breaking the Matthew effect—On women leaving prostitution. *International Journal of Social Welfare, 8*, 67–77.

Matthews, D. (2024). *An exploration of how sex workers who identify as religious or spiritual manage their identities within their everyday lives* [Doctoral dissertation, Nottingham Trent University]. https://irep.ntu.ac.uk/id/eprint/51091/

Mayhew, P., & Mossman, E. (2007). *Exiting prostitution: Models of best practice*. Crime and Justice Research Centre, Victoria University of Wellington. Online: https://www.nzpc.org.nz/pdfs/Mayhew-and-Mossman,-(2007c)-Exiting-Prostitution-Models-of-best-practice.pdf

Network of Sex Work Projects (NSWP). (2024). *Let's talk about sex work: A terminology statement and guide*. Online: https://www.nswp.org/resource/nswp-publications/lets-talk-about-sex-work-terminology-statement-and-guide

O'Neill, M., & Jobe, A. (2022). Sex work, criminalisation and stigma: Towards a feminist criminological imagination. In S. Grace, M. O'Neill, T. Walker, H. King, L. Baldwin, A. Jobe, O. Lynch, F. Measham, K. O'Brien, & V. Seaman (Eds.), *Criminal women: Gender matters* (pp. 63–86). Bristol University Press.

Oselin, S. (2010). Weighing the consequences of a deviant career: Factors leading to an exit from prostitution. *Sociological Perspectives, 53*(4), 527–549. https://doi.org/10.1525/sop.2010.53.4.527

Ouspenski, A. (2014). *Sex work: Transitioning, retiring and exiting*. Ministry of Justice. Online: https://wish-vancouver.net/content/wp-content/uploads/2019/04/SexWork-TRE-REPORT_MAY-6-2015.pdf

Platt, L., Grenfell, P., Meiksin, R., Elmes, J., Sherman, S., Sanders, T., & Crago, A. (2018). Associations between sex work laws and sex workers' health: A systematic review and meta-analysis of quantitative and qualitative studies. *PLoS Medicine, 15*(12), e1002680. https://doi.org/10.1371/journal.pmed.1002680

Prochaska, J., DiClemente, C., & Norcross, J. (1992). In search of how people change: Applications to the addictive behaviors. *American Psychologist, 47*(9), 1102–1114. https://doi.org/10.1037//0003-066x.47.9.1102

Rigney, D. (2010). *The Matthew effect: How advantage begets futher advantage*. Columbia University Press.

Sanders, T. (2007). Becoming an ex-sex worker: Making transitions out of a deviant career. *Feminist Criminology, 2*(1), 74–95. https://doi.org/10.1177/1557085106294845

Sanders, T., Connelly, L., & King, L. (2016). On our own terms: The working conditions of internet-based sex workers in the UK. *Sociological Research Online, 21*(4), 15., http://www.socresonline.org.uk/21/4/15.html. https://doi.org/10.5153/sro.4152

Sandy, L. (2014). *Women and sex work in Cambodia: Blood, sweat and tears*. Routledge.

Scoular, J., & O'Neill, M. (2007). Regulating prostitution: Social inclusion, responsibilization and the politics of prostitution reform. *British Journal of Criminology, 47*(5), 764–778. http://www.jstor.org/stable/23639305

Stella. (2013). Language matters: Talking about sex work. Online: https://www.nswp.org/sites/default/files/StellaInfoSheetLanguageMatters.pdf

Su, Y., & Valiquette, T. (2022). "They kill us trans women": Migration, informal labour, and sex work among trans Venezuelan asylum seekers and undocumented migrants in Brazil during COVID-19. *Anti-Trafficking Review, 19*, 119–124. https://doi.org/10.14197/atr.201222198

Vanwesenbeeck, I. (2017). Sex work criminalization is barking up the wrong tree. *Archives of Sexual Behaviour, 46*, 1631–1640. https://doi.org/10.1007/s10508-017-1008-3

Vanwesenbeeck, I. (1994). *Prostitutes' well-being and risk*. VU Uitgeverij.

Wacquant, L. (1990). Exiting roles or exiting role theory: Critical notes on Ebaugh's becoming an ex. *Acta Sociologica, 33*(4), 397–404. http://www.jstor.org/stable/4200820

Weinhold, C. (2022). *Sex as work: Decriminalisation and the management of brothels in New Zealand*. Palgrave Macmillian.

CHAPTER 3

The Good, the Bad and the Ugly: 'Exiting' Programs, Moral Engineering and Morality Politics

Abstract Globally, 'exiting' programs are one of the key models of support offered to sex workers. In this chapter, we present a series of case studies that describe and explore 'exiting' programs, with examples drawn from a global program review. Shaped and framed by an understanding of sex work as purely harm or trauma and sex workers as exploited victims or deviants, each case study illustrates a particular problematic framing or issue linked to a 'morality politics'. By setting legislative frameworks as the bounded context, our analyses consider the impact of different legislative contexts, including criminalisation, legalisation and the end-demand model (client criminalisation), and uses carceral protectionism as a framework through which to theorise the construction of the vulnerable sex worker as at risk to herself and society in an ever-expanding carceral context. The chapter elucidates how 'exiting' is used in the deployment of punitive and paternalistic responses to sex work and ultimately argues that the discourse of, and practices surrounding 'exiting' capitalises on these constructions to engage in carceral protectionism. Our findings reveal a discourse and practice that perpetuates dominant narratives of sex workers as deviants or victims (or both) and, as criminal or vulnerable, in need of control and protection. Ultimately, we show how 'exiting' programs that view sex work through a harm or deviance lens can operate as a domain of oppression in sex workers' lives.

L. Sandy et al., *Reconceptualizing Exiting and Career Development in Sex Work*, Palgrave Advances in Sex Work Studies,
https://doi.org/10.1007/978-3-032-10077-1_3

Keywords Sex work · Exiting programs · Diversion programs · Stigma · The Swedish Model · Criminalisation · Legalisation · Faith-based exiting programs

3.1 Introduction

'Exiting' programs are one of the key models of support for sex workers. These programs are offered around the world. In this chapter, we share the results of our program analysis that set out to explore best practice in service provision. This work saw us map the sector over a twenty-year period (from 2002 to 2022), where we reviewed 'exiting' programs for evidence in compiling a best practice framework (Sandy et al., 2019a). In adopting a case study design, we present a series of case studies to describe and explore 'exiting' programs, with the examples drawn from our global review of programs. The case studies presented in this chapter each display a particular problematic framing and demonstrate the impact of the shaping and framing of programs discussed in Chapter 2. We undertake this review to highlight the need for academics, practitioners and policy makers to consider the impacts of 'exiting' for sex workers and raise questions about their needs, agency and rights. We have also selected a range of cases that considers the impact of different legislative contexts, ranging from criminalisation in the US to legalisation in the Netherlands and the end-demand model in Canada.

In this chapter, we begin our presentation of the case studies identified during our literature and program review. Each case study is followed by our analysis, in which we used critical content analysis complemented by an evaluation based on specific criteria we developed to establish good practice (see Table 1.2, p.18). In addition to the best practices in sex work programming framework developed through a review of the literature and interviews (i.e., viewing sex work as work, rights-based approach, community empowerment framework, sex worker-led), our 'exiting' program evaluation criteria included: evidence-based program; multiple implementations; independent program evaluation; shown to be effective through rigorous scientific research; and informed by a theory of change. In short, the essential criteria guiding our analysis was evidence and a theoretical basis to the intervention or program (see pages 17–19 for more detail on this). The case studies detailed in this chapter are within the bounded context of the program offered by a particular organisation and the legislative context. We have chosen these contexts as it allows us to concentrate on 'exiting' and the complexities in this area of service provision while elaborating on the influence of conceptual framings on program design and outcomes, which we discussed in Chapter 2, and considering the interplay with sex work laws. It is also a way we can present a rich and holistic understanding of the issue and its many dimensions and aspects. Therefore, in this chapter we set the bounds for the case as the legislative context, as we hope to show how this impacts on the types of programs offered as well as its conceptual framing. This delimits the scope or boundaries of the case: the program, the organisation and the legislative framework. While regulatory models have some use in analysis by enabling us to explain and interpret differences in the varied 'exiting' programs we reviewed, we do not want to convey the idea, or put forward an argument, that regulatory framings or regulatory approaches provide full insight into the issue. Any analysis and understanding of 'exiting' needs to be more than just fitting the models or programs into one or more regulatory models.

Indeed, we hope our analysis helps to reveal how regulatory models are themselves ideological constructs (Agustín, 2008) by illustrating Scoular's (2010) key point that even opposing regulatory frameworks like client criminalisation and legalisation can lead to similar outcomes. We also see this as a way to explore the politics of protectionism underlying mainstream 'exiting' interventions as we unravel the fusing of carceral and protectionist logics to shed light on how sex work policy and programs remain locked in the realm of morality politics (Musto, 2016; Leotti et al., 2023; Rodrigeuz et al., 2020). It is for this reason that most societies do not see 'exiting' programs as a form of intrusion or surveillance but rather as protection and assistance and, when they operate using a sex work as harm or deviance framing, we argue these programs can be a domain of oppression in sex workers' lives, working to exclude access to full and equal citizenship.

3.2 Immoral Deviants/Special Cases: Sex Work 'Exiting' as Social Control

One of the key framings and program logics for 'exiting' programs is sex work as deviance. In this section, we focus on two different legislative contexts, criminalisation and legalisation to highlight how, while the legislative contexts might differ, they are underpinned by similar ideologies. This allows us to illustrate some of the conditions that contribute to sex work policy and programming remaining locked in the realm of morality politics (Wagenaar & Altink, 2012). We begin by exploring 'prostitution diversion programs', using a US-based case study to explore how ideas about recidivism shape 'exiting' program methodologies and evaluation. In comparison to the American program which sees sex workers and clients as criminals, we then consider an 'exiting' program in The Netherlands, funded by the Dutch government. This allows us to explore how 'exiting' programs attempt to regulate 'deviant behaviour' when sex work remains a 'special case' under a legalisationist view (Post et al., 2019).

3.2.1 "Unhooking": Sex Work Diversion Programs

Sex work 'exiting' programs are widely offered as 'prostitution diversion programs' in the US. Broadly speaking, diversion programs are designed to divert people from the criminal justice system. Diversion programs centre around attempting to change behaviour and can happen at different stages of the criminal justice system including prison, probation, or adjudication (Taxman, 2010). Essentially, there are two different forms of diversion programs. The first type is caution or warning programs that divert people away from the criminal justice system with a warning. The second type are formal diversion programs that involve conditions and an agreement to participate in the program. Upon completion of the program, the charges against the person will typically be dropped or no further action will be taken (Wilson & Horge, 2012). Formal diversion programs aim to reduce recidivism by addressing a person's criminogenic needs (Wilson & Horge, 2012). These types of programs tend to connect people to treatment instead of criminal sanctions and are often used to address substance use (Lindquist-Grantz et al., 2021). In the context of sex work and viewing this as deviant behaviour, diversion programs attempt to reduce the 'social problems' said to derive from sex work like creating a nuisance for residents, violence, solicitation and condoms on the street (Leon & Shdaimah, 2012). Sex work diversion programs also attempt to address related issues like homelessness, substance use and mental health concerns (Valente, 2019). Ultimately, the purpose of sex work diversion programs centres on reducing recidivism (i.e., selling sex) by offering sex workers the tools needed to "leave the life" (Valente, 2019, p. 778).

In this case study, we look at a 'prostitution diversion program' in the US, where sex work is criminalised, meaning all practices surrounding sex work are illegal other than some licensed brothels within the rural counties of Nevada (Platt et al., 2018). Across the US, penalties for selling sex include fines of up to US$1,000 and jail sentences of up to one year (Georgia and Nebraska), while other states allow fines of up to $10,000 (Indiana and Texas) or US$25,000 (Illinois) and imprisonment of three or more years for serial convictions (Louisiana and Vermont) (McCarthy et al., 2012, p. 258). Most state legislation considers sex work a misdemeanour, but some states treat first offences as petty (e.g., New Mexico) or a third-degree violation (Pennsylvania), while in other states selling sex is seen as an aggravated misdemeanour (e.g., Iowa) or multiple convictions (three or more) can elevate a subsequent conviction to a felony in states like Florida and Arizona (McCarthy et al., 2012, p. 258). It is important to note that across most of the United States, sexual contact is not necessary for charges, offering or agreeing to perform a sexual act is considered sufficient grounds for charging someone with sex work offences (McCarthy et al., 2012).

The form of criminalisation in the US takes a prohibitionist stance that treats sex work as a criminal issue. Under a prohibitionist view, sex work is seen as an immoral act and sex workers and their clients are viewed as criminals, so need to be legally punished. However, this prohibitionist view has more recently merged with sexual exploitation framings, wherein sex work is conflated with 'sex trafficking' and criminalised. This positioning of sex work as criminal (and deviant) while simultaneously viewing sex workers as trafficking victims translates into how and what types of programs are offered to sex workers and clients. For example, alongside formal sex work diversion programs for women sex workers, clients are usually offered enrolment into a 'John School'—note the language used here which shows the gender bias in sex work laws and programming. These diversion programs are designed to foster self-stigmatisation through which sex workers' clients self-regulate their behaviour (McCarthy et al., 2012). 'John Schools' allow people arrested for buying or attempting to buy sexual services the opportunity to avoid imprisonment or a record if they admit guilt, pay a fine and attend the program (Weitzer, 2011). The programs are said to be rehabilitative; however, they are more focused on blaming and shaming (Fischer et al., 2002; McCarthy et al., 2012; Weitzer, 2011). These diversion programs have been critiqued for their inability to acknowledge sex workers' and clients' autonomy and reinforcing sexual deviance labels (Gurd & O'Brien, 2013). They are also part of the gender ideologies shaping understandings of sex work.

Chicago Prostitution and Trafficking Intervention Court, Cook County State's Attorney, Illinois, United States

Background Beginning in 2015, the Chicago Prostitution and Trafficking Intervention Court (CPTIC) was established to reduce jail overcrowding and encourage sex workers to leave their jobs (Valente, 2019). It is a deferred prosecution program in which participants (known in the program as 'defendants') complete certain requirements in exchange for not being prosecuted (Chicago Alliance Against Sexual Exploitation (CAASE), 2020). According to Valente, the program logics are based on the idea that "prostitution is a crime that many consider a lifestyle, which defendants need to transition out of in order for the commission of crimes to cease" (2019, pp. 777–778). CPTIC allows for sex workers charged with a misdemeanour for soliciting to opt-in the program. They can avoid imprisonment or a record if they successfully complete the program and when a worker graduates, any related charges will be dropped. The program is centred around the idea that sex workers are given the "tools to transition out of the lifestyle" (Valente, 2019, p. 778), and is based on the premise that "those in the sex trade should not be treated like typical criminal defendants but instead offered services and opportunities to exit prostitution" (CAASE, 2020, p. 2).

The Program CPTIC was offered by the State's Attorney Office and Public Offender's Office who worked with service providers (e.g., Salvation Army, Christian Community Health Centres) (Harvey, 2019). The program was created in consultation with the Center for Court Innovation, which is an organisation that "researched and created best practices for human trafficking intervention courts across the country" (CAASE, 2020, p. 16). In the program, sex workers attended specialised female only courts and as 'defendants' they had to attend court otherwise a warrant was issued for their arrest. When they attended court, the 'defendant' was given the opportunity to engage in the program. While participation was said to be voluntary by participants 'opting in', completion of program resulted in dropped charges.

During the court session, the 'defendant' agreed to comply with the program and identified four key needs-based goals. They then completed workshops and goals and along the way, program participants periodically attended court to document progress (if progress towards goals was not met, or the person did not attend court at required intervals, an arrest warrant was issued). If they completed all the set goals, all charges were dropped. According to program statistics, since its inception in 2015 and until September 2019, there were 396 graduates out of 748 enrolled participants (i.e., 53% success rate in program completion) (CAASE, 2020, pp. 16–19).

The most common goal completed was attending "unhooked" classes. These were free workshops offered by Christian Community Health Centres. The workshops focused on supporting participants to apply for jobs and make housing applications. They also offered space for support groups for people to discuss their sex work experiences (read in the program as being trauma and violence) with retired police officers and included presentations from health care professionals about sexual and reproductive health. Other key goals included:

- Completing a HIV test.
- Completing a housing application.
- Completing a mental health screening.
- Obtaining an ID (CAASE, 2020).

There was no assigned time limit to complete these goals, and it could take between one to six months for participants to complete the program; however, some people took two years (CAASE, 2020). If the goals were completed, the charges were dropped and there was a short graduation ceremony where program participants received a certificate and sometimes a backpack with clothes, gift cards and toiletries, all of which came from donations (CAASE, 2020).

In our analysis of program documentation, we could find little evidence suggesting sex worker input into program design. Indeed, the program was created by an organisation known for developing anti-trafficking interventions, which raises questions about the conflation with sex work and trafficking in the program, and offering support groups led by former police officers runs the risk of reinforcing deviance framings and harmful stereotypes. Our analysis of the case study shows that, while this sex work diversion program may adopt an 'opt in' approach, voluntary participation in the program is questionable as the pressure or fear of criminal prosecution remains if they do not engage with the program. There are elements of conditionality for people to engage (to put it simply, if you do not complete the program, you will be charged), and, as people can face fines of up to US$25,000 and subsequent sex work-related offences can become a felony in Illinois, this can act as a form of coercion. It also fails to recognise the structural challenges that can impact on a sex worker's ability to engage in the program's requirements. For example, in the Chicago Alliance Against Sexual Exploitation (CAASE) (2020) report, they note that program participants often have complex needs. This includes substance use and dependency, health issues, complex trauma, housing and economic insecurity, which can also make it difficult for a person to stay in touch with their attorney over phone or get to court. These structural challenges and forms of legal coercion are not addressed in the program, and while program goals may include completing a housing application, the wider issues surrounding this, such as obtaining housing or gaining and sustaining a tenancy are not adequately supported. This can have a significant impact on social security, which can make it more likely for individuals to return to sex work due to the lack of options available (Oselin, 2010; Sanders, 2007). It also does little to address the stigma and discrimination sex workers face in finding housing.

Clearly, post-program employment is important, but getting and staying in work is connected to other challenges, which can include access to stable and appropriate housing, addressing substance use disorders and other mental and physical health issues, where programs are needed both while the person is taking part in CPTIC as well as after program completion. While program goals include applying for jobs, the program itself does little to address the barriers sex workers face in finding secure employment. This includes the stigma of criminalisation and having a criminal record (Hale, 2020), the disconnect program participants may see between sex work and post-program 'square' employment, and personal barriers like limited education and work experience and poor mental health (Baldry, 2010; Franich et al., 2021; Heydon & Naylor, 2018). However, for justice-involved women, many also struggle to find satisfying jobs, which impacts on their ability to attain and retain stable employment (Doyle et al., 2022; Franich et al., 2023). Even if a program participant 'exited' the industry because of the CPTIC, the long-term impact of criminalised stigma would remain a barrier to sex workers obtaining other employment (Naylor & Heydon, 2022).

The core of the program is to encourage workers to leave sex work as part of the State's aim to eradicate it (CAASE, 2020). These stated program aims reinforce sex work stigma by communicating the idea that sex work is inherently bad and something that needs to be stopped. As Gatrell (2010) explains, treating sex workers as needing to change has the potential to impact their social position, and in this way 'exit'-based programs like CPTIC end up reinforcing and compounding stigma as sex work is considered to be immoral. The program goals, then, can be understood as making sex workers normatively moral and responsible citizens as part of the continuing history of regulating and surveilling women's sexuality through the criminal justice system (Corrigan & Shdaimah, 2016; Hannah-Moffat, 2010). Exemplified in this diversion program are thinly disguised moralistic reasons for ending sex work: it is clear that sex work is considered morally reprehensible and a crime, but we can also see some contradictory logics in operation whereby victimisation, agency, rehabilitation and responsibilisation co-exist and remain largely unexamined (Baylson, 2017). What we see in CPTIC is a form of carceral protectionism, where sex work 'exiting' is carried out and experienced through a punitive criminal justice system, with this constructed around the idea of protecting sex workers for their own good (Musto, 2016). The conflation of sex work and sex trafficking in this program means women who are nominally considered 'trafficked', are being arrested, prosecuted and held criminally responsible, leading to incarceration, fines and heightened surveillance—all of which can be avoided by taking part in the diversion program and leaving sex work for good (Baylson, 2017; Musto, 2016). In highlighting these contradictory logics, as Baylson (2017, p. 129) argues, if sex workers are considered as trafficked, this implies victimisation and lack of choice, and if this were the case then, as a trafficked person, they would not meet the criterion of intent (*mens rea*) required for criminal offending. Herein lies the dilemma of 'prostitution diversion programs' that incorporate the dominant, institutionalised gender ideology that women sex workers are 'victim-criminals' (Majic, 2014). In the following section, we explore similar contradictory logics in operation in our examination of another 'exiting' program offered in a country usually considered to have more 'liberal' attitudes about sex work.

3.2.2 *Fixing "Broken" Women: Sex Work 'Exiting' under Legalisation*

The Dutch government legalised sex work in 2000. Legalisation is often seen as a pragmatic approach to regulating sex work, introduced as a harm reduction measure focusing on protecting sex workers' labour rights and health (Weitzer, 2011). In addition to the Netherlands, a number of states in Australia, Germany and rural counties in Nevada (US) have introduced legalisation (Aronowitz, 2014). Under legalisation, most governments implement licensing schemes, with sex work limited to certain areas or sectors of a city. All sex work occurring outside of licensing is said to be illegal and prohibited by law.

The Dutch Ministry of Justice instituted the *Regeling Uitstapporogramma's Prostituees* (RUPS—Exit Programs for Prostitutes) Scheme, in December 2008. The first scheme ran from 2008–2011 and saw the government provide €14.5 million worth of subsidies to municipal authorities and civil society organisations to offer 'exiting' services to sex workers (Regioplan, n.d.). Under the scheme an 'exit' program was defined as "a programme in which prostitutes receive support in finding work or daytime activities not related to prostitution" (Regioplan, n.d., p. 1). The aims of these programs, and the Dutch government funding, was to "coach and support prostitutes wanting to leave the prostitution industry" with "prostitutes ... assisted with problem areas in their lives, such as alcohol/drug dependence, debts, lack of appropriate living space and/or psychosocial problems" (Regioplan, n.d., p. 1).

The introduction of government funded 'exiting' programs came at a time when Dutch legislators started to argue that providing "sexual services directly affected the physical and mental integrity of individuals" (Post et al., 2019, p. 109). RUPS was introduced during a period marked by changing social attitudes towards sex work, from seeing this as a 'normal job' and sex workers as independent and autonomous people working in the industry to victims of exploitation and coercion (Post et al., 2019). This period also saw sweeping changes to legalisation, with the 2007 Coalition government (two Christian parties and the Social Democratic Party) introducing a mandatory and uniform licensing system for sex businesses and client criminalisation when purchasing sexual services from someone under the age of 21 years. The minimum working age for sex workers was increased to 21 and all sex workers were required to register with local authorities. According to the Dutch government, stricter legislation was necessary to address abuses in the sector and protect women who were seen as victims of abuse (Post et al., 2019). This allowed the Dutch government to permit socially acceptable forms of sex work (voluntary work between consenting adults), while seen to be effectively fighting 'damaging' forms of sex work (forced work or minors). We examine the impact of this framing by exploring an 'exiting' program offered by the faith-based organisation *Tot Heil des Volks* (For the Salvation of the People), funded as part of RUPS.

Scharlaken Koord (Scarlet Cord), _Tot Heil des Volks_, Amsterdam, the Netherlands

Background *Scharlaken Koord* (Scarlet Cord) is the 'prostitution service' sitting under *Tot Heil des Volks* (THDV). This Christian aid organisation was founded in Jordaan (Amsterdam) in 1855. The organisation supports the "most vulnerable groups", including "prostitutes", homeless communities, people with substance dependency and children living in poverty (THVD, n.d.). Their motto is:

> Who do you see? Who do you see when you look at a prostitute? Who do you see when you look at a homeless person? Jesus says: 'Whatever you do for them, you do for Me.' When you interact with vulnerable people, you come very close to the heart of Jesus. He identifies with them. In all their brokenness, they reflect something of His pure love. When you see them, you see Him (THVD, n.d.).

Scarlet Cord believes that "every person has been created by God to live in true freedom. In the world of prostitution we see a lack of freedom" (THVD *Scharlaken Koord*, n.d). As such, it aims to help "women and girls who are forced into prostitution" who have interactions with 'loverboys', or 'romeo pimps', which the Dutch government defines as:

> 'Loverboys' (or romeo pimps) are human traffickers who usually operate by trying to make young girls or boys fall in love with them. Sometimes they manipulate young people in other ways. Once they have victims under their influence they exploit them, for instance in the sex industry (Government of the Netherlands, n.d.).

Scarlet Cord have offered 'exiting' services for 35 years and in 2008 they received funding from the Dutch government under RUPS. While RUPS is no longer active, many organisations involved in the scheme, including Scarlet Cord, still offer some form of 'exiting' provision.

The program Scarlet Cord's 'exiting' program was offered to women who work in windows and wanted to stop sex working. Their program worked in the following ways:

- Women received an individual phased plan, dealing at the very least with their financial situation, housing, education or re-education and employment.
- Psycho-social help, aimed at dealing with any (sexual) traumas, building up a social network and how to deal with their feelings and a different lifestyle.
- A case manager as a point of contact (THDV, 2023).

As a part of this service, Scarlet Cord recorded internet-based sex work by scanning Dutch sex websites twice a week, starting in 2016. This monitoring work saw their "digital field team" develop a database in which the organisation recorded "unique profiles" with identifying details that included a worker's name, age, gender, services, location, telephone number, availability, price and level of activity while scanning ads for signs of human trafficking (THDV, 2023). Using these details, Scarlet Cord sent online sex workers text messages, offering support services. In addition to weekly visits to "windows of different red-light districts and sex clubs", Scarlet Cord used this database to locate program participants (THDV *Scharlaken Koord*, n.d.).

According to Scarlet Cord, "women quitting prostitution can receive training at our Work Academy" and the organisation also worked with external partners on sustainable alternative work for people leaving sex work and offered sex workers who want to leave 'buddies' (THDV *Scharlaken Koord*, n.d.). They argued that leaving sex work was an "uncertain time", and "prostitutes can feel guilt, shame, and fear of rejection", which their buddy could help them process (THDV *Scharlaken Koord*, n.d.). Their buddies also took part in social activities or fun things. Alongside this support, they offered workshops and training opportunities and "helping women with practical steps such as making a resume [which] enables them to find new work and have a different source of income" (THDV *Scharlaken Koord*, n.d.). The 2023 annual report documented four women completing training to become 'experienced experts', with one woman securing a paid job and education (THDV, 2023).

In reviewing available program documents, we were unable to find evidence indicating sex worker input into program design. Our analysis of this case study reveals that, while diversity in service provision is important, THDV discriminates on the basis of religion in its employment policies, and the faith component of their organisation can create tension in its delivery and organisational recruitment and structure (Davelaar et al., 2011). As a result, this shapes how they deliver their services as sex workers who are not religious cannot work for the organisation. Religious beliefs on sex work can be negative, and with THDV defining sex work as lacking in "freedom", this then shapes what services are provided and how they are delivered (Matthews, 2024). The organisation also delivers sexuality and prevention lessons in schools, teaching that sex work is morally wrong and the sex industry is a gateway to harm and exploitation (THDV, n.d.). This reinforces sex work stigma and homogenises all people working in the industry as victims.

One positive aspect of this program is offering sex workers training to become experts by experience, which connects to the idea of peer engagement and outreach support to empower sex workers who want to develop their skills and engage in career development. The 'buddy' aspect of the project also has some elements of good practice, as it intends to offer holistic support through supporting workers who go through career changes. However, this is offered within the framing of leaving a bad life behind and starting a new chapter by becoming a morally upstanding member of society. This framing means that support needs are not optimally met as sex work is still associated with morally wrong behaviour and deviance, with workers being encouraged to change 'self-destructive' behaviour. In addition to this, the work of the 'digital field team' in developing a database of online workers for use in recruiting people into the program does not seem to be read or understood by the organisation as infringement of rights or surveillance but rather as offering protection and support, and little evidence is provided for what might count as evidence of human trafficking in sex work adverts.

In both programs, one being a sex work diversion program, another a state-funded, faith-based 'exiting' program, we can see how they are accompanied by punitive elements. In the Chicago program, this takes the form of the threat of fines, incarceration, or a criminal record, while in the Netherlands, this is in increased regulation and surveillance through mandatory licensing, used to 'protect' vulnerable women (we say women here as it is mostly women workers who feature in studies and interventions). These interventions are shaped around protecting vulnerable people from the dangerous (e.g., loverboys and romeo pimps) while also "protecting people from their own danger and for their own good" (Rodriguez et al., 2020, p. 546). This is a form of carceral protectionism we see deployed in punitive and paternalistic responses to sex work and sex workers. Carceral protectionism "relies on a particular understanding of both vulnerability and virtue, employing both law enforcement rescue and coercive 'therapeutic' interventions in order to make particular bodyminds safe and incorruptible" (Rodriguez et al., 2020, p. 538). In these examples of 'exiting' programs we can see how morality politics has fused with a politics of protectionism (Rodriguez et al., 2020). The net effect is that invasive interventions and intrusive measures that force people to leave sex work are not seen as forms of intrusion and surveillance but as protection and assistance (Leotti et al., 2023; Musto, 2016).

3.3 "Socially Tolerated Sexual Predators": Sex Work Exiting as Moral Engineering

Another key framing for 'exiting' programs is sex work as a form of violence against women and girls (VAWG). The modern-day understanding of sex work as a form of violence against women was heavily influenced by Scandinavian research carried out in the late 1980s and early 1990s in which it was argued that "all laws directed against the prostitute ought to be abolished. She is the victim" (Høigård & Finstad, 1992, p. 182; see also Månsson & Hedin, 1999). In this section, we focus on another legislative context resulting from this framing, namely end-demand models (also known as the Swedish or Nordic Model) to again highlight how sex work policy and programming remains locked in the realm of morality politics (Wagenaar & Altink, 2012). This linking is evident in the section title, drawn from Farley who asked: "What shall we call the men who buy the women and children in prostitution? They are socially tolerated sexual predators but are rarely identified as such" (2004, p. 1118). We explore the framing of sex work as violence against women, wherein sex work is said to be rape, and the issues with this approach through a Canadian case study. Heavily influenced by abolitionist feminist arguments about sex work, in 2014 Canada introduced sex purchase laws, seeing the country introduce Janus-faced legislation that criminalised clients while supposedly 'decriminalising' sex workers.

We focus on Canada in this section as it allows us to illustrate the dominant gender ideologies that shape 'exiting' programs under end-demand approaches.

3.3.1 Rescued from "the Game": Sex Work 'Exiting' Under the Swedish Model

The idea behind the Swedish Model is that markets are driven by supply and demand. Here, it is argued that sex work is driven by men's demands to buy sex from women, and if this demand is reduced, sex work can be eradicated (Farley, 2004). Under this abolitionist view, sex work is understood not as the provision of sexual services, but rather as the sale of women themselves, and by its very nature, this cannot be voluntary (Aronowitz, 2014). As a result, all women involved in sex work must be protected as sex work is seen as "incompatible with ideas on freedom of the individual and gender equality" (Aronowitz, 2014, p. 234). In 'end-demand' models, selling sex is legal, but buying sex is illegal. This approach is said to protect workers and target clients. While it is legal to sell sex, brothels are prohibited as are other forms of organised sex work. End-demand approaches have been dubbed the Swedish model as Sweden is noted for its systematic attempts to abolish sex work under sex purchase laws (*sexköpslagen*) (Levy & Jakobsson, 2014). Sweden became the first country to criminalise buying sexual services under sex purchase laws introduced in 1999. 'Exit' programs were a central pillar of policy and programming, with efforts coalescing around social interventions designed to support women leaving sex work developed by the local authorities and civil society organisations.

The framing of sex work as a form of violence against women is problematic, as it relies on essentialised notions of gender and dominant narratives of sex work involving dominant men and submissive women and reinforces the idea that violence against sex workers is inevitable:

> ... we regard prostitution as a particularly hard and brutal oppression, because it has such momentous and long-term consequences for the women. The work of an ordinary wage-earner also wears down the body and soul. But prostitution's destruction of emotional life, self-image, and self-respect is so massive that the comparison with typical waged work grows thin. The long-term harm effected on women who prostitute themselves is similar to that experienced by other victims of sexual violence,

> such as rape and incest victims. It is therefore not mere rhetoric to counter the absurdity of the demand for legalization of prostitution with: "Legalize rape and incest. Recognise these as normal activities" (Høigård & Finstead, 1992, p. 183).

It is a framing that can only see sex workers as victims: recall, "all laws directed against the prostitute ought to be abolished. She is the victim" (Høigård & Finstead, 1992, p. 182), and constructs this as the only legitimate space from which workers can speak about their experiences. This feeds into representations of all sex workers as trapped within a cycle of violence and abuse, and the idea of 'false consciousness' is used to discount the views of women sex workers who may say otherwise as they are unable to see the true nature of their situation. The Swedish model sets out to abolish the sex industry by criminalising the purchase of sex to end demand. It is a criminal justice framing that sees sex workers as victims and clients as criminals, aligning with the belief that sex work is an act of violence against women (Miren & Watson, 2020). We examine the impact of this framing by exploring an 'exiting' program offered by Elizabeth Fry in Canada where sex purchase laws were introduced in 2014.

Exit Doors Here Integrated Care Program, Elizabeth Fry, Toronto, Canada

Background *Exit Doors Here* was a specific service for "sex workers to leave prostitution" offered by Elizabeth Fry in Toronto (Elizabeth Fry, 2020). This organisation also delivered wider services to women and non-binary people who have had challenges with the law including transition housing support, counselling and court programs, employment services and community support programs (Elizabeth Fry, 2020). The *Exit Doors Here* program centres around counselling, social work, cognitive behavioural therapy, skills training, support groups and psycho-education (Public Safety Canada, 2023).

The Program The program objectives were to support women who wished to leave sex work by:

- Strengthening their social support system (through community-based service providers, family members and peers).
- Help support their self-confidence and employability skills.

- Support sex workers progressing towards their goals (Shareck et al., 2024).

The program operated under the Critical Time Intervention (CTI) model. Underpinned by stages of change theory, CTI "is a time-limited evidence-based practice that mobilises support for society's most vulnerable individuals during periods of transition" (Perri et al., 2022, p. 1106). CTI was originally developed to support people who were homeless; however, it has been employed to support domestic violence survivors as well as sex workers (Shareck et al., 2024). According to Shareck and colleagues (2024), the CTI model attempted to keep participants focused and supported, promoted continuity of care, and integrated them into a community network of services aimed at supporting ongoing transition and stabilisation after completing the program over nine months (see also Perri et al., 2022). Program referrals came from outreach workers (meeting clients in the street) and legal, social justice and anti-human trafficking networks. The program was broken up into three three-month phases, which decreased in intensity over time, with program participants working one-to-one with their assigned case manager to co-produce treatment plans tailored to their specific needs. After nine months their case was transferred from their allocated case manager to community support services participants then worked with beyond the nine-month timeframe.

A 2022 evaluation of the program found that the program was successful at reaching the target clients with 95% (n = 52) of participants involved in sex work and 4% (n = 2) deemed 'at risk of returning to sex work' recruited into the program. Follow-up data were available for 30 women and 63% (n = 19) reported they were not involved at all in sex work, while 37% (n = 11) reported they were rarely involved one month after graduating the program. The focus areas for which the most women progressed were support networks with 63% of women (n = 19) reporting progression, followed by accommodation (60%, n = 18), money (50%, n = 17) and work and learning (50%, n = 16). In the program review, Public Safety Canada (2023) noted that participants progressing with work and learning was a positive element of this program as without integrating services that offer economic means through vocational training and job placements for example, the program would not be able to ensure successful exits for workers. In addition to this, Shareck et al.'s (2024) program evaluation noted four key ingredients fostering program success: trust, collaborative goal setting, connecting with community supports and weekly drop-in sessions. It found that the program helped support sex workers to achieve or progress towards their goals, alongside providing other support such as housing. They conclude that 'exiting' programs with an integrated approach encompassing health and social determinants are optimum for successful exits (Shareck et al., 2024).

During our program review, we were unable to uncover any details indicating sex worker input in program design. Our analysis of the case study shows that while there are some notable examples of good practice in this program, as evidenced in Shareck and colleague's (2024) evaluation (e.g., building trusting relationships, collaborative goal setting, connecting with community supports and weekly drop-in sessions) and the use of a theory of change, there are problematic aspects with this program. For example, the evaluation findings acknowledge the non-linear nature of leaving sex work; however, the critical-time-intervention framing and programmatic focus of *Exit Doors Here* focuses on linearity and people quitting sex work and distancing themselves from the sex worker identity "to better their lives" (Valente, 2019, p. 810). Improving sex workers employability skills is an important part of service provision, but this seems to be shaped by the idea that sex workers have little to no confidence or job skills, which reinforces the narrative that workers are needy victims lacking employability skills. Similar to the example of the Scarlet Cord program, under this program, sex workers seem to be 'empowered' through leaving the sex industry and thereby cease being victims.

The framing of sex workers as being 'at risk of returning to sex work', and then measuring this is problematic, as it carries the idea of sex work as a dangerous or harmful activity that people need to avoid. This passes judgement on sex work and sex workers and reveals an underlying logic of controlling women to protect them from what is judged to be a bad or dangerous decision. It also conveys a binaristic understanding of sex work as something a person is 'in' or 'out' of (Bowen, 2015). It may also be problematic for the program to accept referrals from anti-trafficking organisations as the support needs for trafficked persons can be very different, and this also reflects some of the issues with conflating sex work with trafficking. What we can see here is how end-demand models, and the framing of sex work as violence against women results in interventions like *Exit Doors Here*, which rely on essentialist notions of gender that are then "absorbed by institutional regimes in a manner that reinforces, rather than undermines carceral logics" (Leotti et al., 2023, p. 138). The *Exit Doors Here* program offered by Elizabeth Fry clearly sees sex work through an oppression model, offered in a context shaped by abolitionist views wherein women in sex work are seen as victims and the idea of voluntary sex work does not exist, which again firmly locates this area of policy and programming in the field of morality politics (Post et al., 2019). While we do not ignore the fact that some sex workers have benefited from this program, the conflation of trafficking with sex work and idea of sex workers as victims who need to be helped means that sex workers are placed at significant risk of human rights and labour rights abuses, denial of agency and loss of livelihoods (McDermid et al., 2022).

3.4 Conclusion

This chapter has highlighted how 'exiting' programming and policy may incorporate contradictory messages and practices. These programs focus exclusively on leaving the sex industry, a framing encapsulated in the aptly titled program, *Exit Doors Here*, wherein sex work is seen as something women need to escape from. The program framings and abolitionist logics, and subsequent services offered feed into highly individualised understandings of 'personal choice' shaping sex work alongside ideas about victimisation, agency, rehabilitation and responsibilisation. The programs explored in this chapter do little to address the structural issues surrounding some of the reasons people sex work and instead, continue to exacerbate stigma and perpetuate 'deviant' labels, which further compounds stigma and marginalisation.

The in-depth program evaluation undertaken in this chapter revealed some commonly shared elements with organisational practices and programs perpetuating prevailing gender ideologies that see sex working women as 'victim-criminals'. Under a prohibitionist view, sex work criminalisation coupled with the conflation of sex work and trafficking has led to women who are considered 'trafficked' being arrested, prosecuted and held criminally responsible. In this context, sex work 'exiting' becomes a 'get out of jail free' card—'exiting' is carried out and experienced through a punitive criminal justice system. What we see in Scarlet Cord is a program shaped by a prohibitionist view where sex work is considered as immoral and sex workers positioned as victims to be saved (mostly from themselves). The *Exit Doors Here* program sees sex work through an oppression model, shaped by an abolitionist view in which sex work is considered morally repugnant and a threat to gender equality. In all framings, the idea of voluntary sex work does not exist, so sex workers are victims who need to be helped. We have also shown how 'exiting' works as a form of carceral protectionism where sex workers are protected for their own good.

In this chapter, we have shown how various 'exiting' programs are shaped by unabashedly explicit ideologies, which as Wagenaar and Altink (2012) argue, turns this into morality politics. This morality politics, they claim, is "usually a vehicle for a larger moral cause", and to this end we have shown how 'exiting' programs under the guise of criminal justice diversion or anti-trafficking VAWG measures are used as a platform for conservative public order causes (Wagenaar & Altink, 2012, p. 283). Our analyses have shown a remarkable similarity in what is usually taken to be contrasting regulatory approaches. As Scoular (2010) argues, prohibition and legalisation are usually seen as polar opposites, but in each of these framings, the prevailing view of sex work was of moral repugnance and sex workers as victim-criminals who need to be protected. We have shown how supposedly contrasting regulatory approaches have produced the same empirical effects in the context of 'exiting' programs—our findings indicate that, despite "diametrically opposed regulatory approaches", the programs have "produce[d] remarkably similar results on the ground" with this acting as a domain of oppression in sex workers' lives (Scoular, 2010, p. 13). We have also revealed a deep policy conflict between liberal attitudes and morality politics, and the "seemingly irresolvable conflict over deep values" about sex work that sees sex work policy and programs trapped in the realm of morality politics (Wagenaar & Altink, 2012, p. 282). This means that what matters in policy considerations is regulating bodies and sex and not working conditions, and here 'exiting' becomes embroiled in attempts to regulate and control women's bodies and sexuality (Maher et al., 2013).

According to Wagenaar and Altink, good sex work policy and programs "improves the rights—both human rights and labor rights—of sex workers and lessens the negative impact of prostitution on communities" (2012, p. 282). Creating meaningful and respectful relationships between programs and sex workers will remain challenging for services which encourage 'exiting' through criminal justice, deviance or morality framings, for as Wagenaar and Altnik argue, this makes the design and implementation of "effective and humane sex work policy exceedingly difficult" (2012, p. 282). In this chapter, we have highlighted the problems with an 'exiting' mindset, and the issues emanating from this—ranging from sex work being morally and legally wrong or as exploitation, reinforcing the narrative that sex workers are 'trapped in the milieu' and need assistance to leave. The following chapter sheds light on sex workers' views and understandings of 'exiting' programs, as although these services have been provided for a considerable period of time, our analysis has shown how most programs have not been created with sex worker input, meaning they may not be based on needs articulated by sex workers themselves. It has also resulted in a situation where research, theories and programs lack the perspectives, insights and understandings of people with lived experience. This can lead to research and practice disempowering sex workers and the creation of theories, policies and practices that are ineffective, inequitable and unsustainable and, ultimately, may be doing more harm than good.

References

Agustín, L. (2008). Sex and the limits of enlightenment: The irrationality of legal regimes to control prostitution. *Sexuality Research and Social Policy, 5*, 73–86. https://doi.org/10.1525/srsp.2008.5.4.73

Aronowitz, A. (2014). To punish or not to punish: What works in the regulation of the prostitution market. In N. Persăk & G. Vermeulen (Eds.). *Reframing prostitution. From discourse to description, from moralisation to normalisation?* (pp. 223–251). Maklu.

Baldry, E. (2010). Women in transition: From prison to... *Current Issues in Criminal Justice*: *Beyond Prison: Women, Incarceration and Justice*, *22*(2), 253–267. https://doi.org/10.1080/10345329.2010.12035885

Baylson, M. (2017). Victim or criminal? Street-level prostitutes and the criminal justice system. In K. Hail-Jares, C. Shdaimah & C. Leon (Eds.), *Challenging perspectives on street-based sex work* (pp. 136–152). Temple University Press.

Bowen, R. (2015). Squaring up: Experiences of transition from off-street sex work to square work and duality – concurrent involvement in both – in Vancouver, BC.*Canadian Review of Sociology, 52*(4), 429–449. https://doi.org/10.1111/cars.12085

Chicago Alliance Against Sexual Exploitation (CAASE). (2020). *Policing & enforcement of prostitution laws in Chicago.* Online: https://media.nbcchicago.com/2019/09/CAASE-Study.-CPD-Trafficking-Arrests-2020.pdf

Corrigan, R., & Shdaimah, C. (2016). People with secrets: Contesting, constructing, and resisting women's claims about sexualized victimization. *Catholic University Law Review, 65*, 429.

Davelaar, M., van den Toorn, J., de Witte, N., Beaumont, J., & Kuiper, C. (2011). *Faith-based organisations and social exclusion in the Netherlands*. Uitgeverij Acco.

Doyle, C., Yates, S., & Bartels, L. (2022). 'If I don't get a job in six months' time, I can see myself being back in there': Post-prison employment experiences of people in Canberra. *Australian Journal of Social Issues, 57*, 627–648. https://doi.org/10.1002/ajs4.197

Fry, E. (2020). *About*. Online: https://efrytoronto.org/

Farley, M. (2004). "Bad for the body, bad for the heart": Prostitution harms women even if legalized or decriminalized. *Violence against Women, 10*(10), 1087–1125. https://doi.org/10.1177/1077801204268607

Fischer, B., Wortley, S., Webster, C., & Kirst, M. (2002). The socio-legal dynamics and implications of diversion: The case study of the Toronto John School diversion programme for prostitution offenders. *Criminal Justice, 2*(4), 385–410. https://doi.org/10.1177/17488958020020040201

Franich, G., Sandy, L., & Stone., U. (2021). 'It's not designed for women at all': Exploring service providers' perspectives of working in the Victorian criminal justice system. *Current Issues in Criminal Justice, 33*(2), 211–227. https://doi.org/10.1080/10345329.2020.1837713

Franich, G., Sandy, L., & Martinovic, M. (2023, September). *Empowerment through employment for rurally imprisoned women* [Paper presentation]. European Criminology Conference 2023, Florence, Italy.

Gatrell, C. (2010). Who rules the game? An investigation of sex-work, gender, agency and the body. *Gender in Management: An International Journal, 25*(3), 208–226.

Government of the Netherlands. (n.d). *Loverboys*. Online: https://www.government.nl/topics/human-trafficking/romeo-pimps-loverboys

Gurd, A., & O'Brien, E. (2013). Californian 'John schools' and the social construction of prostitution. *Sexuality Research and Social Policy, 10*, 149–158. https://doi.org/10.1007/s13178-013-0117-6

Hale, R. (2020). Good intentions: Women's narratives of post-release anticipatory desistance in the context of historical and contemporary disadvantage and trauma. *Feminist Criminology, 15*(5), 519–544. https://doi.org/10.1177/1557085120923403

Hannah-Moffat, K. (2010). Sacrosanct or flawed: Risk, accountability and gender-responsive penal politics. *Current Issues in Criminal Justice, 22*(2), 193–215. https://doi.org/10.1080/10345329.2010.12035882

Harvey, J. (2019). *A trauma-informed approach for courtrooms handling prostitution-related arrests*. STOP-IT Initiative Against Human Trafficking & Salvation Army. Online: https://centralusa.salvationarmy.org/stopit/news/a-trauma-informed-approach-for-courtrooms-handling-prostitution-related-arrests/

Heydon, G., & Naylor, B. (2018). Criminal record checking and employment: The importance of policy and proximity. *Australian and New Zealand Journal of Criminology, 51*(3), 372–394. https://doi.org/10.1177/0004865817723410

Høigård, C., & Finstad, L. (1992). *Backstreets: Prostitution, money and love* (K. Hanson, N. Sipe & B. Wilson, Trans.). Penn State Press.

Leon, C., & Shdaimah, C. (2012). JUSTifying scrutiny: State power in prostitution diversion programs. *Journal of Poverty, 16*(3), 250–273. https://doi.org/10.1080/10875549.2012.695539

Leotti, S., Muthanna, J., & Anderson-Nathe, B. (2023). Failed mothers, risky children: Carceral protectionism and the social work gaze. *Social Service Review, 97*(1), 130–168. https://doi.org/10.1086/722776

Levy, J., & Jakobsson, P. (2014). Sweden's abolitionist discourse and law: Effects on the dynamics of Swedish sex work and on the lives of Sweden's sex workers. *Criminology & Criminal Justice, 14*(5), 593–607. https://doi.org/10.1177/1748895814528926

Lindquist-Grantz, R., Mallow, P., Dean, L., Lydenberg, M., & Chubinski, J. (2021). Diversion programs for individuals who use substances: A review of the literature. *Journal of Drug Issues, 51*(3), 483–503. https://doi.org/10.1177/00220426211000330

Maher, J., Pickering, S., & Gerard, A. (2013). *Sex work: Labour, mobility, and sexual services.* Routledge.

Majic, S. (2014). Beyond "victim-criminals": Sex workers, nonprofit organizations, and gender ideologies. *Gender & Society, 28*(3), 463–485. https://doi.org/10.1177/0891243214524623

Månsson, S., & Hedin, U. (1999). Breaking the Matthew effect – on women leaving prostitution. *International Journal of Social Welfare, 8*, 67–77. https://doi.org/10.1111/1468-2397.00063

Matthews, D. (2024). *An exploration of how sex workers who identify as religious or spiritual manage their identities within their everyday lives* [Doctoral dissertation, Nottingham Trent University]. https://irep.ntu.ac.uk/id/eprint/51091/

McCarthy, B., Benoit, C., Jansson, M., & Kolar, K. (2012). Regulating sex work: Heterogeneity in legal strategies. *Annual Review of Law and Social Science, 8*(1), 255–271. https://doi.org/10.1146/annurev-lawsocsci-102811-173915

McDermid, J., Murphy, A., McBride, B., Wu, S., Goldenberg, S. M., Shannon, K., & Krüsi, A. (2022). How client criminalisation under end-demand sex work laws shapes the occupational health and safety of sex workers in Metro Vancouver, Canada: A qualitative study. *British Medical Journal Open, 12*(11), Article e061729. https://doi.org/10.1136/bmjopen-2022-061729

Miren, F., & Watson, L. (2020). *The false feminism of criminalising sex workers' clients*. Open Democracy. Online: https://www.opendemocracy.net/en/beyond-trafficking-and-slavery/the-false-feminism-of-criminalising-

Musto, J. (2016). *Control and protect: Collaboration, carceral protection, and domestic sex trafficking in the United States*. University of California Press.

Naylor, B., & Heydon, G. (2022). Criminal records, discrimination, and Aboriginal communities: Enhancing employment opportunities. *Journal of Criminology, 55*(4), 514–531. https://doi.org/10.1177/26338076221128996

Oselin, S. (2010). Weighing the consequences of a deviant career: Factors leading to an exit from prostitution. *Sociological Perspectives*, *53*(4), 527–549. https://doi.org/10.1525/sop.2010.53.4.527

Perri, M., Shareck, M., Buhariwala, P., Hassan, M., Balla, E., & O'Campo, P. (2022). Assessing program fidelity to critically reflect on the suitability of Critical Time Intervention to facilitate exiting sex work. *Translational Behavioral Medicine, 12*(12), 1106–1112. https://doi.org/10.1093/tbm/ibac047

Platt, L., Grenfell, P., Meiksin, R., Elmes, J., Sherman, S., Sanders, T., MwangiI, P., & Crago, A. (2018). Associations between sex work laws and sex workers' health: A systematic review and meta-analysis of quantitative and qualitative studies. *PLoS Medicine, 15*(12), 1–54. https://doi.org/10.1371/journal.Pmed.1002680

Post, C., Brouwer, J., & Vols, M. (2019). Regulation of prostitution in the Netherlands: Liberal dream or growing repression? *European Journal on Criminal Policy and Research, 25*, 99–118. https://doi.org/10.1007/s10610-018-9371-8

Public Safety Canada. (2023). *Exit doors here: Helping sex workers leave prostitution*. Online: https://www.publicsafety.gc.ca/cnt/cntrng-crm/crm-prvntn/nvntr/dtls-en.aspx?i=10184

Regioplan. (n.d.). *Current status of thirteen exit programmes for prostitutes*. Online: https://repository.wodc.nl/bitstream/handle/20.500.12832/2095/2404-summary_tcm28-73360.pdf?sequence=2&isAllowed=y

Rodriguez, S., Ben-Moshe, L., & Rakes, H. (2020). Carceral protectionism and the perpetually (in)vulnerable. *Criminology & Criminal Justice, 20*(5), 537–550. https://doi.org/10.1177/1748895820947450

Sanders, T. (2007). Becoming an ex–sex worker. *Feminist Criminology, 2*(1), 74–95. https://doi.org/10.1177/1557085106294845

Sandy, L., Meenagh, J., & Nes-Iadicola, P. (2019a). *Transitioning programs for sex workers: An exploration of promising practice*. RMIT University.

Sandy, L., Meenagh, J., & Nes-Iadicola, P. (2019b). *Transitioning programs for sex workers: Evidence review report*. RMIT University.

Scoular, J. (2010). What's law got to do with it? How and why law matters in the regulation of sex work. *Journal of Law and Society, 37*(1), 12–39. https://doi.org/10.1111/j.1467-6478.2010.00493.x

Shareck, M., Buhariwala, P., Hassan, M., Balla, E., & O'Campo, P. (2024). Supporting women exit sex work: A contribution analysis of the Exit Doors Here Integrated Care Program in Toronto. Canada. *International Journal of Integrated Care*, *24*(1), 22. https://doi.org/10.5334/ijic.7700

Taxman, F. (2010). Probation and diversion: Is there a place at the table and what should we serve? *Victims & Offenders*, *5*(3), 233–239. https://doi.org/10.1080/15564886.2010.485903

Timmerman, M., Kuin, M., & can Leerdam, J. (2019). *Summary evaluation of exit programmes for prostitutes scheme (RUPS II)*. Online: https://repository.wodc.nl/bitstream/handle/20.500.12832/2413/2943a_summary_tcm28-384792.pdf?sequence=3&isAllowed=y

Tot Heil des Volks (THDV). (2023). *Tot Heil des Volks Annual Report 2023*. THDV. Online: https://thdv2023.jaarverslag.org/dit-is-thdv/

THDV. (n.d.). *English information*. Online: https://www.thdv.nl/english-information

THDV *Scharlaken Koord*. (n.d.). Stop human trafficking and forced prostitution! Online: https://scharlakenkoord.nl/en/what-we-do

Vanwesenbeeck, I. (2017). Sex work criminalization is barking up the wrong tree. *Archives of Sexual Behaviour*, *46*, 1631–1640. https://doi.org/10.1007/s10508-017-1008-3

Valente, B. (2019). Treatment with a side of stigma: The influence of sex work stigma on the Chicago Prostitution and Trafficking Intervention Court. *DePaul Law Review*, *68*, 777–811.

Wagenaar, H., & Altink, S. (2012). Prostitution as morality politics or why it is exceedingly difficult to design and sustain effective prostitution policy. *Sexuality Research and Social Policy*, *9*, 279–292. https://doi.org/10.1007/s13178-012-0095-0

Weitzer, R. (2011). *Legalizing prostitution: From illicit vice to lawful business*. NYU Press.

Wilson, H., & Hoge, R. (2012). The effect of youth diversion programs on recidivism: A meta-analytic review. *Criminal Justice and Behavior*, *40*(5), 497–518. https://doi.org/10.1177/0093854812451089

CHAPTER 4

Changing the Narrative: 'Exiting' and Sex Work Stigma

Abstract In this chapter, we explore the links between stigma and 'exiting' and discuss the challenge of reducing stigma associated with sex work in relation to the dominant framings of 'exiting'. Studies show that stigma is exacerbated by the framing of sex workers as deviant others that often leads to criminalisation. However, there has been little in-depth exploration into the relationship between 'exiting' programs and sex work stigma. Drawing on the findings of in-depth interviews with sex workers and sex worker advocates in Australia and Aotearoa New Zealand, in this chapter we fill a gap in the literature by presenting new empirical data exploring the strained relationship sex workers and advocates have with these programs and how the language of 'exiting' perpetuates stigma. In 'exiting' research, very few studies have considered the voices and views of sex workers and how they understand and view the practice, and this chapter is perhaps one of the first to consider this vexed issue. This chapter addresses a significant gap and offers an alternative framework for analysing 'exiting' that foregrounds the diverse voices and views of sex workers and their supporters which leads us to highlight the problematic framings of respectability underpinning 'exiting'. We see this as part of ongoing work to counter stigmatising narratives and, ultimately, by shedding light on the negative impacts of 'exiting' for sex workers, we illustrate the paradox of these programs as part of our efforts to change theory and practice.

L. Sandy et al., *Reconceptualizing Exiting and Career Development in Sex Work*, Palgrave Advances in Sex Work Studies,
https://doi.org/10.1007/978-3-032-10077-1_4

Keywords Sex work · Criminalisation · Respectability · Exiting · Marginalisation · Meaning

4.1 Introduction

One of the main challenges in understanding people's experiences of leaving sex work stems from the problematic nature of some of the research in this area, which we discussed in Chapters 2 and 3. As we argued in those chapters, most of the research on 'exiting' has been in criminalised contexts, takes an abolitionist approach to sex work and has not been carried out by or for sex workers. For example, Månsson and Hedin (1999) developed the first 'exiting' model for understanding women's experiences of leaving sex work. In Chapter 2, we explored the framing on which they based this model, where women's work in the industry was seen exclusively as exploitative and violent. This, Sanders (2007) claims, leads to a framework that depends upon women's own individual strengths, and as we highlighted in that chapter, this is a questionable premise for any model setting out to understand workers' experiences and the structural and social barriers that shape this. These framings are also problematic as they are based on the view of sex work as purely harm, and therefore, something that needs to be escaped and cannot be a legitimate choice.

In this chapter, we put forward alternative perceptions of 'exiting' programs by presenting the findings of highly original research exploring the voices and views of sex workers and advocates to understand the differing ideas held about these programs. We do so to highlight the difference between sex workers' understandings compared with people outside the industry in the hope of creating awareness of the controversy surrounding this area of service provision. We also do this to push theory to consider how 'exiting' programs are intimately connected with exercising power and control over sex workers and perpetuating stigma and discrimination. In this chapter, we present findings from in-depth interviews with sex workers and allies in Australia and Aotearoa New Zealand. We discussed this method in detail in Chapter 1 (see pp. 8–19 to 19–20), and to briefly recap, twenty-one in-depth interviews were carried out with twenty-eight individual interviewees working with sex worker support organisations providing some form of 'exiting' or transitioning services or programs in Aotearoa New Zealand and Australia (see Table 1.1, pp. 15-16 for a list of participants). The interviews allowed us to understand sex workers' perspectives on 'exiting', which are documented for the first time in this book. These data offer insight into how sex workers and allies made sense of, and understood, this area of service provision.

Throughout the chapter, research participants and organisations are either named, with RMIT University Ethics approval, or assigned a pseudonym. If a participant is not named, only basic information has been provided, and we have done this to protect anonymity. In writing this book we felt it was important to recognise and represent research participants in a way that respected their individual and collective rights and marginalised people's agency while protecting participants against potential harms. Central here was the principle of respect for persons, which is not only key in ethical research, but as Aurini and Iafolla (2023) suggest, asks us to privilege participant autonomy in making decisions about what happens (or not) to them. While well intentioned, some ethical review boards stipulate the use of anonymisation techniques in research to prevent identification (e.g., pseudonyms etc.); however, this can compromise research participants' autonomy and self-determination. We wanted to be mindful of this, especially when researching with sex workers who are part of a marginalised group and in an area of sex work research that has been critiqued for denying sex workers agency and autonomy, seeking to undermine their human rights, and being stigmatising and dehumanising (Green, 2014). For us, providing participants with the opportunity to choose how they were represented in the research was a way to create respectful, community-responsive research that recognised self-determination and supported choices.

The chapter begins with an exploration of sex workers' views about 'exiting', which allows us to unpack some of the key issues with the language of 'exiting'. Here we explore sex workers' perceptions of 'exiting' in interview data, which leads us to argue for a radical change in language and terminology. This sees us tackle the issues surrounding sex work stigma and ideas about sex work and respectability carried in 'exiting' frameworks. We pull apart the discourse of respectability reinforcing societal ideas that sex work and sex workers are not legitimate by documenting sex workers' views and perceptions of the context 'exiting' programs operate in, where sex work is seen as 'unworthy work' and sex workers as 'unworthy subjects'. Here, we contend that ideas about respectability become the reason for an 'exiting industry'. Ultimately, we argue that when sex workers are positioned as unrespectable and unruly subjects, the 'exiting industry' exists as part of societal attempts to make sex workers 'respectable subjects'.

The past two chapters have highlighted how most 'exiting' programs have been developed by people outside of the sex industry. In this chapter, we outline the need for sex worker inclusion in policy and programs. This is because the chapter presents very different views, voices and experiences of 'exiting' that we need to listen to. Through our presentation of highly rich interview data, we reveal the ultimate paradox of exiting, namely, while these programs may be needed because of sex work stigma, 'exiting' itself perpetuates stigma. This, we argue, presents a strong case for the need to reconceptualise 'exiting': we need to change the narrative as our analysis shows problematic framings of respectability underpinning 'exiting'. Our exploration of sex workers' perspectives draws out the dissonance between needs identified by sex workers and those projected on them by others, thereby highlighting the strained relationship some sex workers have with these programs. Listening to sex workers' voices and understanding their frustrations with this area of service delivery has direct relevance for practice, as this can help in developing a more grounded understanding of the role: 'exiting' and 'exiting' programs for sex workers, thereby offering insight into the different value that may be placed on these programs by people working in the industry. It also has direct relevance for research and theory building as we reveal new ways of thinking about the subject.

4.2 "Saving Their Souls": Understanding Sex Workers' Strained Relations with 'Exiting'

'Exiting' programs set out to help sex workers leave the sex industry, and as we showed in Chapter 2, how sex work is conceptualised in these programs can be quite different. In some, sex work is framed as a dangerous and harmful activity that people are either trapped in, escaping, or have survived (Bowen, 2015). When sex work is framed this way, there is an assumption that workers want to leave the industry because engaging in sex work is seen as traumatising. This may be the case for some people doing sex work, but it isn't shared by all, and the problem with this assumption is that it leads to very narrow understandings of 'exiting'. We can see this in the term 'exit' which positions sex work as something that needs to be escaped, and, as we have shown, this leads to a binary understanding of sex work as something that you are either 'in' or 'out' of. This binary works to reinforce the dichotomised ways in which sex work is conceptualised in the 'exiting' literature and programs, where sex workers are "either in, or out, successful or defeated" (Bowen, 2013, p. 89). It also produces a "targeted sympathy" through which certain sex workers come to be deserving victims, supported by seeing sex work as a survival strategy that no one with other options would choose (Leon & Shdaimah, 2021, p. 128). As a part of the 'othering' discourses surrounding sex work, this 'targeted sympathy' works to determine deservingness and shape ideas about ideal subjects and respectability.

On the other hand, when sex work is framed as a 'problem' and criminalised, 'exiting' often takes the form of diversion or rehabilitation programs that dominate criminal justice approaches in which selling sex is highly stigmatised criminal behaviour and sex workers are "contemptible, pathetic and morally deficient" (Leon & Shdaimah, 2021, p. 129). In Chapter 3, we highlighted some of the consequences of the problematic framings in this area of programming and research often designed around moralising ideologies and developed in criminalised contexts. These programs are also designed and delivered in a crimino-legal system that is profoundly sex negative and functions to fix identity, where what someone does (selling sex) defines who they are ('prostitute') and sets them apart as 'other' and 'victim-criminals' (O'Neill, 2010, p. 213; Wodda & Panfill, 2018). In our book so far, we have shown how this results in the contradictory logics seen in 'exiting' programs and interventions. Given this problematic history, it is unsurprising that many sex workers have a fraught relationship with 'exiting' as this is an area of programming and service provision that seeks to permanently 'exit' sex workers from a profession that is not only viewed as harmful and morally wrong but also claimed to be something that any reasonable adult would not choose to do. In this section, we explore some of the resistance sex workers have towards 'exiting' and unpack the reasons for this, connected to disrespectful framings that simplify the diverse employment experiences in sex work and take the view that once you get into sex work, you need to get out—whether you want to or not. We do this by exploring some of the issues with terminology and language raised during interviews with sex workers and sex worker advocates in Australia and Aotearoa New Zealand. These data highlight the different value sex workers place on these programs and unravel the problematic aspects of 'exiting' to illuminate the underlying assumptions about the respectability of sex work and sex workers.

4.2.1 *"We Don't Exit Judges": Understanding the Language of 'Exiting'*

Almost all interview participants spoke about how they found the term 'exiting' offensive, for example, Sarah felt that exiting was a "very negative word. As soon as sex workers, we hear that word, I think many of us feel immediately defensive" (Interview with Sarah). Participants like Sarah spoke about how they believed that non-sex workers saw sex work as, in Sarah's words, "a horrible job" that people wanted to escape from. It is this understanding that creates the need for an 'exiting industry' designed to help people leave sex work. During interviews, participants highlighted how the term 'exiting' and framing of programs was counterintuitive to understanding sex work as work. This was a fundamental point of resistance to 'exiting' for some sex workers:

> I wouldn't use [the term exiting] ... I think it's fundamental that people have to realise that sex work is actual work and that's a difficult concept for a lot of people to grasp. Talking about an exiting program where no other industry has exiting programs, we don't exit judges, lawyers, politicians, plumbers, anybody like that (Interview with Michael).

For P.G. Macioti, a former outreach coordinator in Berlin-based Hydra e.V., the term 'exiting' had "a negative connotation ... linked to problems of addiction rather than changing jobs". This was because:

> the vast majority of [sex workers] see their activity as work, even if they don't identify as sex workers, would feel this term as stigmatising, and as referring to their work as not work, but as something that is desirable to leave behind, which is part of the problem for people who would like to do other jobs alongside sex work or stop doing sex work. So [other people] not seeing it as work is part of the crucial problem that hinders mobility in the labour market (Interview with P.G. Macioti, University of Technology Sydney (UTS), University of Western Australia (UWA) & Hydra e.V. (Berlin)).

P.G. Macioti highlights how sex workers see 'exiting' as part of the objectifying and dehumanising narratives applied to sex work and, while she saw the term as inherently stigmatising, it also perpetuated the myths and norms surrounding sex work and sex workers. Ahi Wi-Hongi from the New Zealand Prostitutes Collective (NZPC) also saw the term as part of the stigmatising language surrounding sex work and sex workers:

> ... it's one of those words that makes it seem like sex work is so different to other kinds of work, I've never been asked about exiting factory work or other jobs that I've done ... it's really stigmatising language (Interview with Ahi Wi-Hongi, NZPC).

Catherine Healy also from NZPC outlined the ways in which the term had "become quite loaded", and in her perspective, it shared ties with conservative approaches, which was a key reason for rejecting the concept: "It's sort of an anti-sex worker approach, the word exiting is not generally – I don't think it's used in any other occupational context and for that reason I find it very clumsy and offensive actually" (Interview with Catherine Healy, NZPC). Lexxie Jury, an outreach worker on the Sex Worker Outreach Program in the Australian Capital Territory (SWOP ACT) rejected 'exiting' as, for her, it was intimately connected to ideas about sex workers as 'fallen women' and discourses of redemption and sexual purity, and the saviour complex:

> If you want – if you don't want this to be seen as a saviour, a saving of sex workers, saving of their souls, saving of their purity; if you don't want it to seem like that, you need to change the terminology, it needs to be called something else. It needs to be called – I don't know, anything is better than an exiting program. Immediately, I just come back to I don't want to talk to you (Interview with Lexxie Jury, SWOP ACT).

In expressing opposition to 'exiting', Jules Kim, CEO of Scarlet Alliance, Australia's national sex worker association, not only shared these views but explained how the approach redirected attention from the sex workers' rights movement and crucial resources:

> [exiting is] problematic terminology in terms of sex worker rights and that's because of that history of exit programs taking money away from sex worker organisations; also, it being seen as this framework that sex work is inherently problematic and that people should be exiting, that that

> is the goal for sex workers … 'exit program' has become so loaded because of past history, that it becomes quite problematic in that context (Interview with Jules Kim, Scarlet Alliance, Australian Sex Workers Association).

When asked about their views on 'exiting' programs, interview participants show the strained relationship sex workers had with 'exiting'. This is because many participants perceived exiting as associated with anti-sex work, abolitionist framings, and to saviour discourses and approaches. We have clearly shown the ideological linking with these framings in Chapters 2 and 3, which warrants these observations. Our interview data extends this discussion by shedding light on the controversy surrounding 'exiting' from a sex worker's point of view and how they saw this as linked to objectifying and dehumanising narratives about sex work. All participants were clear about the importance of defining sex work as work, and many felt this was important to do in 'exiting' programs as it meant that a person's involvement in the industry became a part of that person's working life, and as we continue to explore below, their career trajectories. Moreover, sex workers' resistance to 'exiting' centred upon the 'othering' of sex work and sex workers in 'exiting' discourse. The language and discourse of 'exiting' works to reinforce sex workers as a class apart and as we have shown, this further compounds stigma and marginalisation.

The fraught relationship sex workers have with 'exiting' needs to be considered as part of the issues surrounding language. Our analysis shows it is imperative that these stigmatising discourses are challenged as part of our effort to change attitudes towards sex work and tackle stigma and discrimination. For example, Lexxie Jury's rejection of 'exiting' is due to the close relationship this area of programming has with restrictive and moralistic images of sex workers as passive victims, which she sees as feeding into the idea of rescuing and rehabilitating sex workers. Her emotions are clear and present, and demonstrative of the strong emotions some workers feel about this area of service provision, "I don't want to talk to you", as are her demands: *change the narrative*.

4.2.2 *"One-Way Door": Talking About Leaving Sex Work*

Reflecting on the 'in' or 'out' binary in 'exiting' frameworks, 'exiting' was a problematic term for some participants because of the finality of the word. For example, Michael explained how "[exit] means a one-way door". As a result, he felt the term did not capture or adequately reflect working realities:

> to me it means exit, you're leaving the building sort of thing; there's a fire or something behind you and you know bang you're out and you're not going to come back in through that door, is the sort of way we interpret it (Interview with Michael).

Amelia also spoke about understanding 'exiting' as being an ending:

> ... exiting would mean retiring or going into another job entirely that's not sex-work related ... [it] is like yes, we're ending it here and we're moving onto something else, straight away. I'm not very keen on [exiting], I much prefer transitioning because it's broader and less stigmatising. I think a lot of people hear the old 'exit the industry' and yeah, I just don't like it. I know a lot of sex workers don't. The whole 'exit' pathway. It's transitioning that can encompass building of additional skills, et cetera, et cetera rather than just getting out (Interview with Amelia).

Likewise, for Georgie, 'exiting' had a finality associated with it that failed to capture sex workers' experiences:

> For me personally, it's about someone choosing to look at an alternative work industry. So, they're exiting work. It doesn't mean that they're closing and deadlocking that door ... [for some workers] they were burned out, which happens in careers. So, they felt that choosing to work in [sex work] wasn't an active choice [anymore]. It was an ultimatum, because they'd created a lifestyle they had to service, as we all do. We've all got mortgages or rent and outgoings (Interview with Georgie).

Catherine Healy echoed Georgie and Ameila's point about how 'exiting' did not reflect everyday realities and experiences:

> ... just looking at that word and its connotations and its ownership where it sits predominantly, it's too loaded for us and it doesn't fit with what we see in terms of daily experience, well, you know, what people are talking about when they want to leave. They want to leave, they talk about leaving (Interview with Catherine Healy, NZPC).

These data show that sex workers clearly reject the in/out binary used in theorisations about, and discussions of their profession in 'exiting' literature. This 'in/out' binary encourages the rescue approach we see in 'exiting' programs and we have shown how this was one of the key reasons why sex workers objected to this discourse and approach. Participants were clear that sex work was something a person did not need to be 'in' or 'out' of as the 'exiting' literature suggests, or that they needed saving, thus challenging ideas about participation/non-participation and rescue/redemption shaping conventional understandings of sex work. It is paramount for research, policy and programs to recognise this, for as Bowen argues:

> depicting sex work as something merely to be escaped is a limiting framework that suppresses the experiences of those who live sex work as work; those who supplement square work with sex work; and those who view sex work as an opportunity to ameliorate structural oppressions such as patriarchy, capitalism, and colonialism experienced as gender inequality, poverty and racism (2015, p. 434).

Sex workers were clear that the narrow framing of sex work in 'exiting' discourse failed to capture their diverse experiences, wants and needs. Our findings show the importance of reframing sex work, not as part of morality politics and gendered inequalities tied to heterosexuality, but as work and thus social inequalities related to gendered labouring conditions shaped by intersecting structures like race, ethnicity, migration, age, sexuality, abilities and so on. Here, we have shown how the reframing of sex work as work in 'exiting' discourse can be achieved by listening to and incorporating sex workers' voices, and doing this offers the possibility of moving beyond the victimisation framework currently shaping approaches in research and practice.

4.2.3 *"Almost heresy"? Providing Support Services for Workers*

There is an understandably high degree of resistance felt by sex workers with the term 'exiting', and so far, we have highlighted some of the reasons why. It is important to understand this because, as we argue it leads to frameworks that are unable to fully comprehend workers' experiences, but also, as Alison suggested, this resistance can lead to service provision and programming in this area being "almost heresy". Yet, as she noted:

> If you take the perspective that sex work is work and therefore there's no reason to ever leave it, then you're not treating sex work as work, you're treating it as something completely separate and different and special in some way. Actually, it's work like any other and there is absolutely no reason why you wouldn't want to leave it, just as you may want to leave any other job (Interview with Alison).

Sarah shared these views:

> [Sex work is] like any other job, that if you're not happy doing that job, you change jobs. I've been a waitress in the past; I don't want to be a waitress right now because I have options that I'd much prefer to do. But maybe in the future, if I need to make some money, I'll go back to it. It's the same with sex work. People move in and out all the time depending on their life circumstances and what's working for them at different points ... we don't believe that people should aspire to leave the industry. We believe that people should aspire to do whatever's right for them. If that is leaving, great, we'll help them. But if that's staying and making sure that they're maximising their health and safety while they're working, then that's right up our alley too (Interview with Sarah).

Gabby Skelsey, an outreach worker with Melbourne-based Resourcing Health and Education in the Sex Industry (RhED), raised a similar point when saying that "some workers, like any job, they want to change it" and adopting a rights-based approach can perhaps offer a way to acknowledge and address this in a less problematic framing (Interview with Gabby Skelsey, RhED).

Reflecting on practices in the sector, Jill Martin, a health educator at RhED highlighted how most organisations providing services to sex workers across Australia and Aotearoa New Zealand were engaged in this work:

> Exiting is extremely negative. It indicates that people need to get out of the industry and its often how anti-sex work organisations would refer to a transitioning program. That's not to say that peer-based orgs don't all have some sort of transitioning program, which is at a minimal about workshopping what you're already doing and moving to other sectors of the industry. Generally, all of them will help you with resume writing, getting into that mainstream employment (Interview with Jill Martin, RhED).

Gabby Skelsey shared these views:

> … I don't like the word exit, just because it makes us sound like a saving organisation. Some programs that work with sex workers assume that people who work in the industry are victims of violence. [Our program] is about transitioning or looking at other options, when it's right for the sex worker, in their time (Interview with Gabby Skelsey, RhED).

The contention some participants felt with offering these services was clearly expressed by Ava when she said: "how can we do this within a sex worker rights program framework and yet be supporting people in leaving?" During our interview, Ava spoke at length about how her organisation struggled with language, framing and terminology, eventually settling on transitioning:

> … we never use ['exiting'] in our day-to-day work. It's not used in any of our terminology, it's not used in our resources, none of our promotional tools. There is language around – I think the term is transitioning, if people want to look at the option of transitioning in or out or around sex work. So, it's really just saying to people, this is your career and so you can go which way you want to go (Interview with Ava).

In addition to considering terminology, Georgie reflected on the importance of how these services are delivered:

> … rescue models don't work for me because I'm like, you're assuming someone needs or wants to be rescued, and how dare you! How dare you place that on someone! We have no right to do that. It's a voluntary program and there are some people that absolutely love doing what they do, but they're preached upon … [and] it doesn't always have to be this negative. On the flipside, there are people who have suffered a lot of trauma in and out of sex work and that needs to be acknowledged and supported, too. I think sometimes that's where the disparity is when you're working in a political setting … acknowledging someone's trauma and violence that they've often encountered doesn't mean that you're discounting sex work is real work (Interview with Georgie).

Participants were clear about the need for the meaningful inclusion of sex workers in program design and delivery. Here we have started to sketch out the beginnings of what program and service delivery might look like when it is developed from the voices and views of sex workers and the importance of this being rights-based and person-centred. What we have shown here is a need to focus on supporting choices and empowering workers—this means supporting sex workers to make informed decisions based on the principle of free choice, and this includes the decision to stay in sex work. Non-sex worker-centred methodologies can result in research and practice where power is exercised over sex workers, and they are seen as passive objects and targets for interventions developed by people who are said to have a better understanding of their needs, which, as our interview data demonstrates, many not be the case.

In this section, our findings have uncovered sex workers' resistance to this area of programming, leading to new meanings about 'exiting' through which we can question taken-for-granted assumptions. We have also highlighted the crucial need to work with groups that are directly affected by these programs. This is because we lack more nuanced understandings and approaches better able to meet sex workers' diverse needs. We have also shown how sex workers' and advocates' thoughts, feelings and emotions about the language of 'exiting' can offer us unique insight into both the emotional and interpretive processes (Quinn et al., 2024). In this sense, we have illustrated how sex workers made sense of 'exiting', the problems they saw with this area of programming and, by extension, the actions we can take to remedy this, or as Lexxie Jury advises, it is time we changed the narrative. The renewed emphasis we are seeing with government initiatives and funding for this area of programming and service delivery means that understanding and listening to these voices and views becomes of paramount importance. Bowen argues that "hearing from sex workers is essential to advancing agendas in this area", and our findings show the reasons why this matters (2015, p. 1). In the following section, we continue unpacking the assumptions surrounding exiting uncovered during interviews with sex workers and advocates focusing on ideas of respectability and creating respectable subjects, leading to what we argue is the ultimate paradox of 'exiting'.

4.3 "Ground Zero": Creating Respectable Subjects

In Chapter 2, we provided an overview of how exiting programs developed, and in Chapter 3, we unpacked some of the logics informing these programs. Recall here Fuchs Ebaugh's (1988) work on *Becoming an Ex: The Process of Role Exit*, in which she explored the processes by which people in different circumstances—including former sex workers—left their roles. In Chapter 2, we showed how Fuchs Ebaugh's role-exit theory was influential in the development of 'exiting' programs; however, as we argued, some of the ways that it was engaged with were problematic. For example, Månsson and Hedin (1999) built on the idea of role-exit when developing their theory for understanding how women 'breakaway from prostitution', which continued with the use of highly individualised framings of personal choice in sex work research by placing the onus on the worker's own emotional commitment as the determining factor in leaving sex work. In Chapter 3, we discussed how 'exiting' models ignored the interplay between individual agency and structural factors, thereby constructing sex workers as victims, but in this section, we reveal another issue underpinning these models, namely the assumptions about the respectability of sex work and sex workers informing 'exiting'.

In our analysis of the literature on 'exiting' and during interviews, the issues surrounding respectability became apparent. Most of the literature focuses on street-based sex work: workers with 'chaotic lives' and backgrounds of social disadvantage, trauma, and abuse. While these are the experiences of some sex workers, over representation in 'exiting' research (and sex work research more generally) feeds into the stigma and discrimination that sex workers face. Specifically, in relation to 'becoming an ex', the literature and theoretical frameworks place significant emphasis upon experiences of trauma and loss (sometimes framed as 'hitting bottom') as creating a catalyst for exiting and reinforcing the idea that sex workers have nothing to contribute or occupy some kind of 'ground zero'. In this section, we explore the impact of this framing, and consider this in relation to ideas about respect, respectability and making respectable subjects.

4.3.1 *"If You Were a Good Girl": Respectability and the Legacy and Logics of 'Exiting'*

One of the main critiques of 'exiting' was the assumptions surrounding respectability built into programs. For example, when reflecting on how she saw 'exiting' programs as being shaped by the views and concerns of non-sex working people, Jane Green from the Melbourne-based sex worker organisation, the Vixen Collective, highlighted some of the assumptions sex workers are met with, and that inform 'exiting' programs:

> I think there's a lot of the ideas of other people outside sex work and particularly people that work in other services have this perception that

> we've only ever done sex work. Therefore, we need some massive amount of help to do something else ... or they have this perception that sex work is not skilled work, and we have no skills. Therefore, we need to learn skills or be trained to do anything because we're starting from some sort of ground zero where we have nothing. Neither of those things are true and that's really problematic.... and workers tend to find that's really offensive (Interview with Jane Green, Vixen Collective).

This discourse of respectability was reflected upon by Sarah:

> We recently advertised for a position, and we put that sex work experience was desirable, but we didn't put it as essential. I noticed all the non-sex workers who applied were so much more confident in their ability and talking themselves up. All the sex workers who applied, who were fairly easily matched on skills, qualifications, everything, were so much less likely to imagine that they would get the job or be considered for a role and things like that. That confidence goes a long way in job seeking. That's not because they're not skilled, it's because they have this perception that others won't think that they're skilled enough (Interview with Sarah).

Lexxie Jury shows how some sex workers viewed the term 'exiting' as connected to the idea of saving women—from themselves:

> I have to say, when I first read that you wanted to do an interview about this, it really got my hackles up and I was like actually just calm down, deep breaths. For me it brings – it raises the people that want to save us, that we'll teach you how to sew because that is such a better job than what you're doing ... it goes back to that judgement, you can't fend for yourself, so we'll teach you how to, we'll give you some kind of skill so that you can move on from here and we can save you from this life. That's what it dredges up for me ... if you were a good girl, we would never have gotten into this situation in the first place... if you – if we just help you get better, like I'm sick, we can concentrate on that and we can make it better and we can save you, we can fix it (Interview with Lexxie Jury, SWOP ACT).

While care was taken with the drafting of the Participant Information Sheet and Consent Form, Lexxie Jury's response to the invitation to participate in the research shows just how infuriated she was about this area of programming. For Lexxie Jury, this centred on ideas about public credibility and, in being misrecognised as pathological, the relationship between sex work, identity and respectability: "If you were a good girl, [you] would never have gotten into this situation in the first place". Her emotions are raw and real: 'exiting' programs infantilise sex workers, discredit their life choices and devalue their experiences. 'Exiting' programs question a sex worker's decision-making abilities and social and cultural competency—they 'other' sex workers and devalue their lives and work. Sarah's story where she shared an example of job recruitment in which sex work experience was advertised as desirable, and sex worker candidates were evenly matched on skills with non-sex worker candidates shows how sex workers interviewed for the role felt. When compared on equal terms with other workers, sex workers' responses reveal stigma, and the effects of internal stigma, social stigma, structural stigma and whorephobia: their skills were not seen as legitimate because of societal ideas that sex work, and by association, sex workers are not legitimate. Our interview data shows that it was these underlying assumptions about respectability in 'exiting' programs that sex workers felt most at odds with.

During interviews, participants made it clear how these programs connected with broader cultural narratives and systems of oppression that 'other' sex workers and differently frame them through lenses of what, and who counts as respectable (Meenagh & Sandy, 2018; Skeggs, 2005). Participants clearly outlined the context 'exiting' programs operate in, and this is a context that does not ascribe value or worth to sex work, as Jane Green reminds us, a "ground zero" where sex workers "have nothing" of value. In 'exiting' frameworks and approaches, sex work becomes 'unworthy work', and understood as being work without value, by association, sex workers become unworthy subjects (Meenagh & Sandy, 2018). As we argued in Chapter 2, these types of framings abound in the literature because most research has been carried out without sex worker collaboration or input and comes from contexts where sex work is criminalised. In countries with sex purchase laws (e.g., Canada and Sweden), or in the US, and to a lesser extent the UK, the government reinforces 'exiting' through rehabilitation or diversion from incarceration. This carceral framing is not concerned with recognising transferable skills or career development, instead it assumes an undisciplined, unskilled and unruly subject.

4.3.2 *The 'Exiting' Paradox...*

We ended our interviews with a question reflecting on the potential for sex worker specific transitioning programs to be useful, and the hesitancy that some sex workers have towards engaging with them. We did this by asking participants the following question: If we take the perspective that sex work is work, is a program that specifically focuses on transitioning from the sex industry necessary? Most, but not all, participants responded yes, but this wasn't about workers lacking key skills, as P.G. Macioti reflected, it was "because of stigma, yeah, and because of criminalisation, yeah. It's not necessary, it's wished for. It's helpful" (Interview with P.G. Macioti, UTS, UWA & Hydra e.V., Berlin). This view was shared by Jill Martin: "Unfortunately, yes. Yeah, once more stigma and discrimination. Just that lack of access to mainstream employment once you've just outed yourself as a sex worker, sort of thing" (Interview with Jill Martin, RhED). Gabby Skelsey reflected on this question by expanding on some key points:

> Look, I think I'm going to come down and say yes, because of the stigma and discrimination that sex workers face. It is very challenging for them to find a space where they can talk about what's going on for them and be given the opportunity of supporting them to leave the industry, so I think yes, yeah, I think it is (Interview with Gabby Skelsey, RhED).

Although Sarah didn't agree with these views, she did highlight similar systemic issues faced by sex workers: "No, I hate it, it's so patronising. It's disgusting, yeah ... [we need] advocacy for decriminalisation, community education to reduce stigma and discrimination, and empowerment programs for sex workers" (Interview with Sarah). Sarah's vehement "no, I hate it", shows participants' deep feelings about and emotional engagement with this area of service delivery.

Some participants, however, were conflicted in their response to this question. For example, Charlotte answered this question by saying:

> It's counterintuitive. I think having a transitioning program is counterintuitive to understanding that sex work is labour ... in a political sense, we do damage, this program existing – any of these types of programs existing. In saying that, our program has validity, though. It does. It does. I think our program does assist, but in a different way. I think any type of transitioning program – particularly the way we work it, and the way

> our attitudes are as a collective whole, is that we provide flexibility. We provide understanding. It's voluntary. We don't push our agenda. I think that what we can do is listen to people that come to us wanting certain things, and wanting support for certain things, and we give it ... sex work as labour though? [Exiting] fucks it up (Interview with Charlotte).

For Olivia, while the conflict was "difficult" for her "to sit with", she likewise saw the need for these services because of stigma and criminalisation:

> There's that conflicted space that I – I feel conflicted with ... I find it difficult to sit with, in the sense that, you'd hope that in an environment where you do have a regulated system, where there is less stigma attached to it, that you wouldn't need a program like this for people, but on the other hand, the reality is that there is still a lot of stigma attached to the industry and I think it is a bit of a struggle, yeah (Interview with Olivia).

In answering this provocation, Amelia and Lexxie Jury encapsulated the diametrically opposed views about this area of service provision:

> Absolutely. People want to transition from one career choice to another all the time. It's that simple. I used to be a chef, hated it and went and did retraining into nursing. Hated that as well, but let's not go there. Yeah, people make career transitions all the time and it doesn't mean that they're previous career wasn't work, it just means that it's not fitting for them anymore for whatever reason (Interview with Amelia).

> That's a really good question ... I guess that's where my dislike of exiting, transition, like there's no other job in the world what has an exiting or transitioning position. I don't ever – as a SWOP outreach worker, no one's offering me a transitioning job, no one's offering me an exiting job. As a bank teller, as a cop, as a lawyer, as anything, nobody else is offered that. You get offered upskilling, I guess, that kind of thing as my job here at SWOP, but there's no – that doesn't happen kind of anywhere else. It's only as a sex worker that we're going to offer you a transitioning or an exiting program (Interview with Lexxie Jury, SWOP ACT).

Although not everyone agreed with the need for a specific 'exiting' program to address this issue, almost all participants agreed on the systemic factors that needed to be addressed: stigma and discrimination, legal change, skilling and upskilling and retraining support. Further, these data reveal the tensions felt by some people providing these services in sex worker support organisations. In our interviews, this conflict and emotional engagement was ever present, yet almost all participants identified a need for support services in this area. However, some questioned if an entire program was necessary. For many, there was an agreement on the needs for support, but the reason for this was because of the stigma and discrimination sex workers faced and this becomes the paradox. What emerges from our findings is the need for these programs to engage in advocacy to challenge perceptions of sex work as not being skilled work. The programmatic logic of 'exiting' renders sex work as work unintelligible, leading to rescue-based approaches and sex work abolition.

At the crux of sex workers' responses to program need was addressing stigma and discrimination and law reform as some of the reasons why workers find it difficult to leave. Here, our analysis highlights how participants countered dominant narratives, leading to the argument that support was needed because of sex work stigma and not as sex workers lacked key skills. This sentiment was echoed by some participants, who noted that 'exiting' programs tend to be designed and developed by people outside of the industry, which we confirmed in the program analysis presented in Chapter 3. Arguably, if sex work is a job like any other there should not be a need for these services targeted directly at sex workers. However, because of the stigma and discrimination that surrounds sex work the need for sex work specific services exists, and ultimately, this is the paradox of 'exiting'.

4.4 Conclusion

This chapter has furthered a critical understanding and appreciation of 'exiting' by presenting sex workers' resistance to this area of service provision. We have done this by examining how sex workers made sense of 'exiting' and shown what this illustrates about an emotionally and politically charged terrain of service delivery and the fraught relationship sex workers have with 'exiting'. Our findings elucidate sex workers' and advocates' perspectives of 'exiting' and, further building on Chapter 3, we have enriched our understandings of the consequences of these programs. Our analysis centred these situated knowledges to help in explaining the resistance sex workers have to this specific area of programming, thereby building knowledge in this area while also highlighting sex workers' needs. By situating sex workers' voices and views at the centre, we have created a more nuanced understanding of 'exiting' and the harms of existing frameworks and approaches, and raised awareness of the dissonance that exists between needs identified by sex workers as opposed to needs projected on them by people outside of the industry. In this way, we argue, we can make sense of the harms that accompany sex work criminalisation and 'exiting' programs. However, this 'exiting' industry prompts some important questions sex workers raise about this programmatic area: why do sex workers need an 'exiting' industry, and support for transitioning into a different career?

For perhaps the first time in publication, these interviews have allowed sex workers to express their exasperations and frustrations with policy and funding decisions that define their realties and working experiences and in which they have had little direct input. Clearly, support is needed because of stigma—stigma makes it hard to move out of sex work, and ideas about 'exiting' reinforce stigma when sex work is not seen as valid work and sex workers are cast as unworthy subjects. This suggests then, the need to recognise the complexity and difficulties faced with language and terminology and the importance of developing a definition and framework based on the idea of sexual labour and sex worker agency, which is a core feature of understanding sex work as work. In this chapter, we have not only made a clear case for the importance of transforming theory and practice but have also highlighted the paradox of 'exiting': these programs are needed because of the stigma surrounding sex work, and this stigma exists because of moralising ideologies and criminalising legislation.

In the next chapter, we show how many sex workers and sex worker support organisations engage in this work, and because of this, there is a need to work on language and frameworks to ensure we develop programs and services that do not perpetuate stigmatisation and marginalisation but rather support free choice, sex worker self-determination and autonomy. We need to do this work, because as we have shown, problematic conceptualisations of respectability shape ideas about 'exiting' and the kinds of services and programs offered in this area, some of which may not be fit for purpose. In the chapters so far, we have unpacked some of the reasons why these problematic framings exist and slowly unravelled the consequences, but now we must ask ourselves, if there is a need for these services, how can we avoid this? In the following chapter, we continue our examination of 'exiting' in practice, by exploring this through the lens of labour market practices and working conditions and do so to illustrate how considering 'exiting' from a labour perspective offers insight into how sex workers themselves understand and view the practice, thus offering alternative frameworks through which we can begin to reconceptualise 'exiting', which is the project of this book.

References

Aurini, J., & Iafolla, V. (2023). Who owns your consent? How REBs give away participants' agency. *Research Ethics, 19*(4), 474–493. https://doi.org/10.1177/17470161231180829

Bowen, R. (2013). *They walk among us: Sex work exiting, re-entry and duality* [Masters dissertation, Simon Fraser University].

Bowen, R. (2015). Squaring up: Experiences of transition from off-street sex work to square work and duality – concurrent involvement in both – in Vancouver, BC. *Canadian Review of Sociology, 52*(4), 429–449. https://doi.org/10.1111/cars.12085

Fuchs Ebaugh, H. (1988). *Becoming an ex: The process of role exit.* University of Chicago Press.

Green. J. (2014). Listen to sex workers – you'll realise we have a lot to say about labour rights. *The Guardian* (29 September). https://www.theguardian.com/commentisfree/2014/sep/29/listen-to-sex-workers-youll-realise-we-have-a-lot-to-say-about-labour-rights

Leon, C., & Shdaimah, C. (2021). Targeted sympathy in "whore court": Criminal justice actors' perceptions of prostitution diversion programs. *Law & Policy, 43*(2), 126–148. https://doi.org/10.1111/lapo.12166

Månsson, S., & Hedin, U. (1999). Breaking the Matthew effect - on women leaving prostitution. *International Journal of Social Welfare, 8*, 67–77. https://doi.org/10.1111/1468-2397.00063

Meenagh, J., & Sandy, L. (2018, November). *Exiting assumptions: The problem of respectability in transitioning services for sex workers* [Paper presentation]. Australian Sociology Conference 2018, Deakin University, Melbourne, Australia.

O'Neill, M. (2010). Cultural criminology and sex work: Resisting regulation through radical democracy and participatory action research (PAR). *Journal of Law and Society, 37*(1), 210–232. https://doi.org/10.1111/j.1467-6478.2010.00502.x

Quinn, K., Buck, G., & Tomczak, P. (2024). Mobilizing metaphors in criminological analysis: A case study of emotions in the penal voluntary sector. *British Journal of Criminology, 64*(6), 1239–1258. https://doi.org/10.1093/bjc/azae027

Sanders, T. (2007). Becoming an ex-sex worker: Making transitions out of a deviant career. *Feminist Criminology, 2*(1), 74–95. https://doi.org/10.1177/1557085106294845

Skeggs, B. (2005). The making of class and gender through visualizing moral subject formation. *Sociology, 39*(5), 965–982. https://doi.org/10.1177/0038038505058381

Wodda, A., & Panfil, V. (2018). Insert sexy title here: Moving toward a sex-positive criminology. *Feminist Criminology, 13*(5), 583–608. https://doi.org/10.1177/1557085117693088

CHAPTER 5

Beyond the Binary: Understanding 'Exiting' Practices in Sex Work

Abstract This chapter explores sex workers experiences with leaving sex work. This includes the research documenting their formal engagements in and with 'exiting' programs and their own working practices. By exploring the research in this area, we create a picture of how sex workers 'exit' or disengage with sex work, but do this from the perspective of labour market conditions and employment practices, and a broader consideration of stigma and discrimination that includes intra-occupational forms of stigma. Ultimately, the chapter highlights the misalignment of sex workers' diverse experiences with current theories and frameworks, allowing us to consider alternative framings more apt at capturing their lived experiences.

Keywords Sex work · Exiting decisions · Re-conceptualising 'exiting' · Marginalisation · Criminalisation · Career planning

5.1 Introduction

In sex work research, there is a substantial body of literature exploring the reasons for people starting sex work (see, for example, Barry, 1995; Bishop & Robinson, 1998; Busza, 2004; Campbell, 2003; Chapkis,

L. Sandy et al., *Reconceptualizing Exiting and Career Development in Sex Work*, Palgrave Advances in Sex Work Studies,
https://doi.org/10.1007/978-3-032-10077-1_5

1997; Day, 2007; Derks, 2008; Farley, 2007; Ford & Lyons, 2011; Kempadoo, 1999; Kulick, 1998; Lim & ILO, 1998; Murray, 2001; Norma & Tankard-Reist, 2016; Parreñas, 2011; Sanders, 2005; Sandy, 2014; Wardlow, 2006; Wojcicki, 2002). While not all research frames motivations for sex work within the prism of sex work as a social problem or a form of violence against women, as Mayhew and Mossman (2007) suggest, there is a large evidence base that argues people (predominately women) enter sex work because of damaged or inadequate social backgrounds (see, for example, Barry, 1995; Bindel et al., 2012; Brown, 2000; Farley, 2007; Månsson & Hedin, 1999; Norma & Tankard-Reist, 2016; Oselin, 2010). As we have shown in our other chapters, this perspective leads to the assumption that sex workers want to leave the industry because engaging in sex work is seen as harmful and dangerous behaviour that causes trauma. For example, Williamson and Folaron state that for street-based sex workers: "it is the sum total of daily hassles, acute traumas, and chronic conditions that precipitate a woman's decision to exit prostitution" (2003, p. 283). As Law argues, these studies tend to view "exiting as trauma recovery", and as a result, some of the studies do not consider sex work to be a form of labour (2013, p. 105, for examples of 'exiting' as trauma recovery see Hedin and Månsson (2004), Månsson and Hedin (1999), Oselin (2010) and Williamson and Folaron (2003)). However, there is also a growing body of work that argues people start sex work to make a living and see this as a way to meet the challenges of precarious financial situations and structural oppressions (see, for example, Benoit et al. (2018), Bowen (2021), Chapkis (1997), Day (2007), Law (2000), Lim & ILO (1998), Sanders (2005) and Sandy (2014)). This literature puts forward the idea of sex work as work and this framing encourages us to explore how we can understand people's diverse employment experiences within sex work. In this chapter, we explore sex workers' experiences in formal 'exiting' programs, conditional 'exiting' structures and their self-exiting practices. We have shown the wide range of 'exiting' programs offered to sex workers, but as demonstrated in Chapters 2 and 3, these have been built on ideas of sex work as exploitative or deviant and something that workers need to be saved from or stop doing.

Drawing on evaluative studies of formal 'exiting' programs, or research studies with sex workers about their 'exiting' experiences, we continue our efforts to unpack problematic framings in this area of research, while also drawing on a small body of work exploring sex workers personal strategies for leaving sex work. We do this to highlight workers' diverse experiences and understand how sex workers 'exit' or disengage with the sex industry. By exploring sex workers' perspectives of the labour market and working conditions and practices we consider catalysts that may lead to sex workers wanting to leave the industry. This includes ideas about 'hitting bottom' or 'turning points' identified in the 'exiting' literature or violence and religious or spiritual reasons, after which we look at how sex workers develop their own informal 'exiting' plans and rationales for these. While this chapter does not present new research or data, our analyses explore sex workers' own informal practices to highlight the misalignments with formal 'exiting' programs discussed in Chapters 2 and 3. We present these new analyses as part our effort to reconceptualise 'exiting', and as a way for us to consider the idea of career development and progression in sex work and thus develop a novel framework grounded in lived experiences.

5.2 Reasons for Leaving

Most 'exiting' studies focus on people's reasons for leaving and it is here that we also see some of the more problematic framings of sex workers' experiences in these studies. Some of this is based on research with workers in formal 'exiting' programs, while other studies document informal practices in the sector. We begin this part of the chapter by critically analysing sex workers' experiences of 'hitting bottom' and going through a turning point event as a reason to leave the industry. Experiences of violence and hostility follows, which link to turning points of change; however, our analyses offer a more nuanced understanding of the impact stigma and safety has on sex workers' decisions to leave the industry. Finally, we explore how sex workers connecting to religiosity can be a catalyst to change their identities and behaviour through leaving sex work.

5.2.1 *"Hitting Bottom": Exploring Cumulative Burdens*

'Exiting'-specific studies have identified some of the reasons for women wanting to leave sex work, including cumulative burdens. In research with street-based 'prostituted women' in the US, Dalla (2006) explored motivations for leaving sex work which she labelled as 'hitting bottom'. Dalla reported four out of five participants "hit bottom", which she explained as significant events culminating in a woman's decision to stop sex working, including being viciously attacked by clients, losing custody of their children due to substance use, or going to prison (2006, p. 280). For example, in Dalla's (2006) study Amy described 'hitting bottom' when she lost custody of her children due to her addiction to crack cocaine. This was a gradual process for Amy as losing her children led to increased drug use. However, she did engage with an in-house drug program, which she explained was because the "CPS [Child Protective Services] made me… They said, 'you have to go to treatment to get your kids back'" (Dalla, 2006, p. 280).

According to Dalla:

> Rachel also described hitting bottom. She was sentenced to prison for 4 years on multiple drug and solicitation charges: "As much as I hate to say it", she remarked, "something good comes out of something bad. Prison did save my life. It really did. I was out there killin' myself" (Dalla, 2006, p. 280).

Dalla goes on to say that, at the time of imprisonment, Rachel "had a $500/day addiction to crack cocaine and had nearly overdosed on three separate occasions", leaving no doubt that Rachel 'hit bottom' due to her substance use disorder (2006, p. 280). Dalla notes that three out of the four participants she categorised as 'hitting bottom' had attempted to leave sex work before, and their current disengagement was noted as "successfully avoiding the sex industry, substance use, and criminal activity for a significant amount of time" (2006, p. 281).

Given that sex work is seen in almost exclusively negative terms in most 'exiting' studies, it is important to critically reflect on terms like 'hitting bottom' when describing the experiences of street-based sex workers. While we are not taking away the traumatic challenges described by Dalla (2006), as the participants in her study were engaging in personal struggles, the idea of 'hitting bottom' suggests that the women in her study could not get any lower and were in the worst possible state. While terms like 'hitting bottom' are used in the literature, this language and framing is rarely applied to indoor workers. In this way, these sorts of framings can be classist and patronising to sex workers and work not only to reinforce hierarchical systems within the sex industry but also further compound sex work stigma and perpetuate harmful stereotypes. 'Hitting bottom' reinforces negative perceptions of sex work and street-based work, which is a heavily stigmatised form of sex work.

When this is seen in the context of stigmatisation that also takes place within sex work and the internal dynamics of stigma that privilege more socially acceptable forms of sex work, the idea of 'hitting bottom' also reinforces the whorearchy (Toubiana & Ruebottom, 2022). This intra-occupational stigma hierarchy is based on physical (corporeality of the work (e.g., contact/non-contact sexual services)), demographic (socioeconomic status, race etc.) and moral (rationales for sex work) stigma (Toubiana & Ruebottom, 2022). As an example of this within street-based sex work, in Dalla's (2006) study, Marlee said she left sex work because of the declining economic viability. Marlee's reflections, however, drew on this intra-occupational stigma hierarchy:

> The girls out there now are not like we used to be. They're out there for drugs. That's why the business is so bad. It's not even worth it. They're crack heads and will do anything for a little bit of money... they're not real ones [prostitutes]" (Dalla, 2006, p. 281).

Here we can see an internal ranking in operation based on more or less stigmatised positions, moral judgements and demographics: street-based sex workers who use drugs are at the very bottom of the hierarchy. Marlee uses this stigma hierarchy not only to distance herself from more stigmatised groups and but also avoid being stigmatised. What we can see here is a secondary ordering in this intra-occupational stigma hierarchy whereby workers who are on the same level of the hierarchy based on physical stigma (e.g., street-based sex workers) can and do make moral judgements about workers lower in the hierarchy (Toubiana & Ruebottom, 2022). For Marlee, she detaches "crack heads" as outside of the occupation "they're not real ones", yet her comments show how stigmatisation can come from inside the industry. This reveals how this stigma may differ as well as the role 'exiting' programs may play in perpetuating this internal stigma hierarchy. Furthermore, ideas of 'hitting bottom' feed into the stigma hierarchy, both by sex workers and wider society, where there is also a hierarchical ranking of sex work based on agency and choice and sex work as empowering or harmful (Puffer et al., 2024). Likewise, viewing women's participation in sex work as 'successfully avoiding' the sex industry reinforces a deviant identity, which can negatively impact sex workers' experiences while working, and if they change careers. While 'exiting' provisions must be able to provide support for the challenges described by these sex workers (e.g., substance use support), this must be offered with respect and acknowledgement of the possibility for workers re-entering the sex industry and consideration of this within the sex work stigma hierarchy. As Gesser and Shdaimah (2021) note, return to sex work should not be viewed as a failure and should be met non-judgmentally, and framings of 'successfully avoiding' sex work carries judgement about the work.

5.2.2 *"Turning Points": Catalysts for Change*

Månsson and Hedin first identified turning points in their 1999 study of street-based sex work in Sweden. Turning points may include traumatic events (e.g., violence) or what they term as "positive" life events like relationships and children (Månsson & Hedin, 1999, p. 71; Oselin, 2010). Oselin (2010, p. 536) also identified arrests and prison, hospitalisation, pregnancy and childbirth as turning points, and argued that, after going through a turning point event, women's reasons for leaving often become more salient. Oselin (2010) found similar motivations for women leaving street-based sex work in the US, but added fatigue from working on the streets, becoming sober, other relationship factors (e.g., new romantic partner or re-establishing connections with family and/or friends) and lack of sexual interest in men (e.g., conflicting sexual orientation, lack of sexual pleasure) as factors for leaving sex work. For Oselin, it was not the presence of these factors alone that facilitated transitions as often the goal of leaving sex work was accompanied by a "turning point of change" (2010, p. 536). Oselin defined turning points as various reasons women decide to leave sex work including being arrested, hospitalisation and pregnancy/childbirth (2010, p. 536).

Sanders' (2007) study with indoor and outdoor workers in the UK found that a worker's individual reasons for leaving sex work and turning points were often connected, and sometimes the same; however, Oselin disagreed with this finding. Although Oselin (2010) provides examples where there is an overlap, the women in Oselin's study tended to see these as two distinct categories, thus showing that while the reasons and turning point events may often be similar, sex workers themselves may not necessarily view them as being the same. The reasons for leaving and turning point event can be two separate, but interconnected things. For example, a person's reason for leaving sex work may be violence and/or exhaustion and the turning point event could be witnessing or experiencing excessive violence. While these seem similar, workers may understand them as separate events, with the turning point event acting as a catalyst. Furthermore, the women in Oselin's study cited reasons for leaving that varied from their turning point event, which led her to argue that experiencing a turning point event gave prominence to their reasons for leaving. For example, one of the women in Oseiln's study, Shondra, stated that her reasons for leaving sex work were religious beliefs and fear of violence; however, what acted as a catalyst for Shondra was being arrested and placed in prison (turning point event). She explained:

> God finally rescued me the last time I went to jail, and it finally clicked after I was arrested that this was God's way of helping me out. I prayed for God to strengthen my faith in Him and to put Him in my life... to feel what I knew was right and what I was raised to believe in. I embraced that and ran with it because that was my lifeline and I knew with no doubt in my mind that if I would have kept going the way I was going I would end up dead. After I was released I went right into the program because I knew this was my one shot (Oselin, 2010, p. 537).

For Tisha, escalating violence and being "burned out" were the key reasons why she wanted to leave; but for Oselin (2010, p. 537) it was the re-arrest and possibility of substantial jail time that was identified as a turning point:

> I was on parole and I got busted for prostitution again. I knew I was going back to prison for a long time, so I called my parole officer and asked her to recommend me for Phoenix instead. At that point, I knew something had to change. I got lucky, instead of returning to prison, I got a chance to go there (Oselin, 2010, p. 537).

It should be noted that when commenting on burnout, participants in Law's (2013) study with indoor sex workers in Toronto and Montreal insisted that burnout was not unmanageable or specific to sex work. Burnout, rather, was compounded by stigma, with workers describing the "psychological toll of 'a life of secrecy' ... and 'terrible shame' about doing sex work" (Law, 2013, p. 102).

5.2.3 *"It Was Bad Out There": Violence and Hostility*

Sanders (2007) found some common reasons for leaving sex work shared by all workers, including the fear of violence and hostility. A common experience for the women in her study was leaving in response to a specific violent attack at work or the general increase in violence and hostility sex workers encountered. Similarly, Dalla (2006) noted exposure to violence as a major reason for wanting to leave sex work. In her study, Yolanda and Kiley spoke about wanting to leave after "they were viciously attacked by clients; neither thought she would survive" (Dalla, 2006, p. 280). Yolanda entered a 12-month residential drug and mental health treatment program immediately after being attacked, whereas for Kiley, this was a gradual process; however, her experience of violence initiated her decision to leave:

> I just got tired. I started going to detox more frequently. Then, the last time [at detox], it just happened like that [snaps fingers]. I just reached out and asked if there was a bed in long-term care (Dalla, 2006, p. 280).

Sex working women in Oselin's study expressed similar sentiments. For example, Jenna said:

> I was almost killed by my last john, and I ran for my life. I know I needed to get help, but I couldn't stop. It was bad out there … I was raped many times and left for dead, having people cut my face up and damage my eye (Oselin, 2010, p. 533).

What this research shows is that the combination of socio-legal contexts that criminalise sex work and drug use, coupled with arrests and violence both complicated and shaped 'exiting' and reasons for leaving sex work. This was particularly so for workers who had involvement with the criminal justice system because of criminalisation and also experienced high levels of violence and drug addiction. Some of these studies, however, framed sex work as deviance, and sex workers as having a 'deviant identity', and this means they may not necessarily consider the role and impact of stigma and stigma management in shaping working experiences. While prison may be a space for some people to reflect, this is not a trauma-informed setting and can potentially be harmful. It is also not an optimal setting to plan and develop skills that may be needed once a person has decided to stop sex working. Additionally, the levels of hostility and violence reported by people sex working in criminalised settings, means that, for some, sex work was no longer viable because they were fearful of violence, which can be said to be a forced 'exit'—if harm reduction strategies like working together to enhance safety or sex work decriminalisation were in place, this may impact on a person's decision to leave. This kind of 'exit' can have a profound impact on sex workers' physical and mental health while also placing them at risk of economic vulnerability because of their forced disengagement from sex work. These experiences show the need to reform sex work laws and include career development services within programs, including career upskilling, help with governmental or state financial support, and therapy to navigate these experiences that can be catalysts for leaving sex work.

5.2.4 *"A Pillar of the Community": Adopting a New Mindset*

Another noted influence in people's decision to leave the sex industry was religious and spiritual reasons (Dalla, 2006). Sex workers who engaged with religiously affiliated formal 'exiting' programs were motivated to stop 'immoral behaviour' and become a respectable member of society through adopting often Christian values and morals (Deer et al., 2021). By doing this, sex workers were noted to change their mindset, lifestyle, views, and subsequently, their identities (Deer et al., 2021).

In Dalla's (2006) study, three out of five participants had ascribed religious identities from childhood, but during their adulthood, religiosity became central in their lives. For example, after release from prison, Rachel found that religion had become a central part of her life: "I'm not a Bible thumper—but I look at my kids, I look at my husband, I look at where I was, and I've got God so much in my life right now. I couldn't do it without Him. I really couldn't" (Dalla, 2006, p. 283). Amy described a similar journey when a co-resident at a treatment facility introduced her to religion, which had a profound impact:

> I was always talking about my kids and wondering if they were okay and blah, blah, blah and she told me 'You need to give your kids to God because you can't take care of them. You never did take care of them.' And it was sad, but it was true. I learned I had to focus on myself and my recovery. In order for me to be a whole person, I had to recover first (Dalla, 2006, p. 283).

Clearly, Amy adopted a new mindset in relation to religiosity, which then became a key motivation for leaving sex work. Participants in Deer and colleagues (2021) study also adopted a new mindset, which saw them leave the "lifestyle" associated with sex work and "start over entirely":

> You have to give up everything—any cars you have, any places you live, friends you may have that are associated with, anybody who is trying to keep you in the life. You basically fall off the face of the earth for a *while*...That's what's been harder. Knowing you have to start over (Jillian cited in Deer et al., 2021, p. 5).

In their research, Clara was described as "not being able to see the chaos in her lifestyle" (Deer et al., 2021, p. 6); however, after engaging in a religiously affiliated 'exiting' program, Clara said:

> I remember somebody asking me about the unmanageability of my life. And I was like, 'My life's not unmanageable.' She said, 'You are 34 years old. Do you have a bank account?' No. 'Do you have a car?' No. 'Do you have a place to live?' 'Yeah, that house.' 'That's a homeless shelter...So your life's unmanageable.' I'm like, 'Nah, I don't see that.' I felt like I was managing my life (Deer et al., 2021, p. 6).

Following the support received while on the program, Deer and colleagues (2021, p. 6) stated that Clara was able to see "her prior life more clearly" as she had a bank account and her own place. Here we can see a more natural progression out of sex work, in that Clara desired a new lifestyle after taking part in the program (Sanders, 2007). Identity transformation was an experience noted by Deer and colleagues (2021), with the participants in their study adopting what they labelled "mainstream identities":

> Well, I mean, I would have been an ex-crackhead prostitute, that didn't, you know, scum of the earth is how I felt about myself, that's for sure. Addict, again. But now I'm a wife, a mother, a business owner, I'm a sinner, I'm a saint. You know, like, I'm a friend and a pillar of the community (Clara cited in Deer et al., 2021, p. 7).

A key finding in their study was that religiosity offered participants access to these mainstream identities and new support systems with friends from their church, through which they could become a part of the faith-based community (Deer et al., 2021). Involvement with the church was a central theme in their transitions out of sex work, with some participants using this as a way to distance themselves from sex work and the sex work community. However, what we can see with this kind of natural progression out of sex work is how it can work to reinforce negative attitudes about sex work and sex workers as 'immoral' or wrong. This is reflected in some of the comments about sex work made by participants in Dalla's (2006) and Deer and colleagues' (2021) studies, along with their arguments about sex workers needing to adopt mainstream identities and practices to be seen as successful.

Sex work negativity is an important point as it can be challenging for sex workers who are not religiously orientated or hold a religious belief, when they engage in these types of services. For example, Gloria said that religious organisations needed to "let people be who they need to be in that moment, without ramming religion down their throat and truly embracing in a nonjudgmental, compassionate, client-centred way" (Deer et al., 2021, p. 7). However, for Eva, the curfew, Church attendance, Bible study and restoration with family required by the program gave her the structure she felt she needed:

> So long as you're living [at the organization] you have to live a certain way. You can't be living here and trying to do that [sex trade] too... So, there's these rules that you have to follow and when things come to the light, then you've got to go. You know, no hard feelings, but if you don't want to live that way then go back to doing what you were doing (Deer et al., 2021, p. 8).

Clearly, how religious organisations offered support was just as important as the support they offered, and this also played a role in shaping people's reasons for, and experiences of, leaving sex work. It also plays a role in how sex workers make sense of 'exiting', for example, in Deer, Zarestky and Baumgarther's (2021) study, participants were recruited by religiously affiliated (Christian) non-profit organisations. Nine out of the ten women in their study were helped to leave sex work by these organisations, and one was assisted by another 'exiting' organisation in a different US state, but it is not clear if this was a religious organisation. The negative views participants held towards sex work could be part of adopting 'mainstream identities' and reflective of the views held by these organisations, researchers and wider society. For example, Gloria talked about "the 'bling-bling' of the sex trade", which Deer, Zarestky and Baumgarther (2021) interpreted as being like "an addiction ... [with women] romanticizing their past experiences" in the early stages of the program:

> You try to make it a positive thing when really it's not. You try to legitimize it to yourself. It wasn't that bad, but when you really start sitting down and thinking about it. No, no, it was really that bad. *Why am I trying to put glitter on it and call it something it's not?* There's a difference between war stories and reminiscing and romancing it…but guess what's the reality of this? You're putting a dick in your mouth for a purse (Jillian cited in Deer et al., 2021, p. 6).

While Jillian may have experienced abuse and trauma at work, this passage shows how some women made sense of and talked about leaving sex work, possibly influenced by the profound sex negativity in some 'exiting' programs and research. Clara demonstrates how, as a former sex worker, she came to internalise these negative attitudes, which she first learnt through the women working in the organisation:

> I was really honest early on, TOO honest. And [the support organization leaders] would be like, 'Watch what you're saying now, because one day you are going to have a life and you're not going to want that everywhere around.' And I'm like, 'Nah, I'm good girl, I'm good'…And I get that today. I'm like, 'Yeah, I don't want everyone to know that.' But I didn't get that then…[Now] I don't self-disclose like that…like nobody at my gym, nobody at my work. They don't know anything. They just know me as, she's getting her master's degree, she's married, basic stuff (Deer et al., 2021, p. 7).

These observations are important because in their study Deer and colleagues make extensive comments on how the women learnt new behaviours and identities by "observing and emulating behaviors as a means of integrating into society"—as if the women were not members of society before leaving sex work—but some of the women's reflections on this process reveal how they began looking down on their peers and developing whorephobic attitudes as a part of entering 'mainstream' society:

> Well, watching women like [women working at the organization] and the way they dress and understanding that they were not showing their boobs

> to everyone and they did not have a whale tail [G-string] up the back. And I was like, 'Hold on, hmmm, classy, not classy, classy, not classy'. Starting to look at what was appropriate. So, I think it was just by really being observant... One of the girls showed up with a john one day and she was trying to pull her clothes on as she was coming into the computer class. And I was like, hmmm, do I want to be that girl, or do I want to look like [women working at the organization] (Clara cited in Deer et al., 2021, p. 8).

Matthews' (2024) research with religious and spiritual sex workers in the US and UK shows there may be a role for religious organisations as participants in her study highly valued their religious and spiritual identity. Therefore, some sex workers may want to be in services which are religiously orientated, as this aligns with their various identities, but this support needs to be person-centred and non-judgemental, and in some instances the research shows that this may not be the case.

5.3 Beyond In/Out: Exploring Sex Workers' Career Planning

Many studies have documented the temporary nature of sex work, and while some people's engagement in sex work may be short-term, this is not the case for all workers. In this section, we explore some of the everyday working practices that help manage why workers might leave, while also considering how they plan for the temporary nature of sex work. We introduce this analytical framing to challenge the prevailing idea of sex workers needing to leave a 'deviant identity', and instead explore economic viability and working conditions as reasons for leaving or staying in sex work and managing precarity. Following this, we look at how sex workers attempting to optimise their income, work-life balance and work-related benefits such as healthcare or pension contributions shapes their engagement with sex work. By exploring how sex workers set short-, medium- and long-term goals, prepare for exclusion from the sex industry and engage in financial planning, we show the complexity of, and diverse engagements they have with sex work.

5.3.1 *Preparing for Precarity*

It is important to recognise that many people see sex work as temporary. For some workers, mobility or movement in, out and within sex work is a part of the work and their expected employment trajectories (Ham & Gilmour, 2016). Many studies with sex workers have documented how they do not see the job as something they will do forever, for some they plan to sex work for a short period of time or to meet certain goals (Bowen, 2021; Brennan, 2004; Chapkis, 1997; Day, 2007; Groves et al., 2008; Ham & Gilmour, 2016; Law, 2000; Sanders, 2005; Sandy, 2014). For example, Ham and Gilmour (2016) noted that the participants in their study started escort work to finance specific goals, fund specific purchases or be able to study or work while their children were young. Maher et al. (2012) and Sandy (2014) noted financial benefits, flexibility, the ready availability of work and the temporary nature of it as key reasons for sex working. Because of these perceived advantages of sex work, almost all workers in Ham and Gilmour's (2016) study reported needing to prepare themselves for living without secure well-paid work.

The precarity surrounding sex work extended to the need to prepare for potential exclusion from sex work. For example, Ham and Gilmour documented a narrative where some workers felt the need to ensure they were in a "position to leave the industry before it left you", and some the factors they identified as impacting on career longevity included age, gender, class and ethnicity (2016, p. 5). Dalla (2006), Sanders (2007) and Oselin (2010) also noted workers feeling too old or psychologically or physically fatigued as a key motivation for leaving sex work. Oselin discussed how workers "claimed to feel the tangible effects of [their] years on the streets" (2010, p. 533). Amy told Oselin that:

> I was tired of prostituting, yeah I wanted to try and change my life, but I was having a hard time doing it anymore.... So I came here [to a residential exiting program], to try and get out of it and off the streets, so I could do something else because I'm getting way too old for it (Oselin, 2010, p. 533).

According to Drucker and Nieri (2018) this was an issue for some online workers. For example, Polly said "she would stop advertising when 'my prime's done' because she did not want to compete with younger sex workers and feared that she would get burned out" (Drucker & Nieri, 2018, p. 7). For others this may not be about burn out, but economic conditions. In Dalla's work, Marlee spoke about leaving sex work because of declining economic viability: "The girls out there now are not liked we used to be. They're out there for drugs. That's why business is so bad. It's not even worth it" (2006, pp. 280–281). What this shows is how leaving sex work is seen as an "expected development" and a natural progression (Gilmour, 2020, p. 304).

In some of these studies, worker's stories do not really involve a significant identity shift or turning point, like we see being argued in frameworks using stages of change or role-exit theories. For example, in Ham and Gilmour's (2016) study with migrant and racialised women working in the indoor industry in Melbourne (Australia) and Vancouver (Canada), sex workers understood and explained 'exiting' more as a personal or professional strategy. In this research, as Gilmour argues, some sex workers will "always intend to transition out of the industry at some point, no matter how positive their experience of the industry may be, because it is an industry in which there are diminished returns with advancing age" (2020, p. 304).

These studies with diverse sex workers raise several important points relevant to career development and progression in the industry. This includes self-perceptions of people's engagement in sex work as potentially being time-limited and how people managed precarity in their lives, which is reflected in employment patterns and high levels of mobility in, out and within the industry. For example, the most significant form of worker mobility documented by Pickering, Maher and Gerard (2009) was movement in and out of Melbourne's sex industry. Only seven out of fifty-five workers interviewed in their research had never stopped sex working and most of the participants in their study saw sex work as supplementing other forms of employment and life activities (Pickering et al., 2009, p. 9). Here, they noted how some workers had dual careers, with sex work supplementing or supporting other careers and workers moving into and out of the industry on that basis (Pickering et al., 2009, p. 8; see also Ham and Gilmour (2016, pp. 6–8)). Bowen (2015) expanded on this idea of dual carers when documenting how workers in Vancouver engaged in 'square' (non-sex work) jobs alongside sex working. In Bowen's study, participants worked simultaneously in sex work and 'square' work, which was a way to reduce burnout and frustration and find a balance between working just enough in sex work to get the income needed, and not so much that it caused burnout or frustration (Bowen, 2015, p. 440). In these studies, sex workers engaged in dual careers where sex work was a way to get additional income while working in 'square' jobs, and for some, this working arrangement was seen as the best way to do sex work.

5.3.2 *Fluid Engagements with Sex Work*

Challenging binary understandings of sex work as something you or in or out of, in Drucker and Nieri's (2018) study on 'exit planning' for online workers they claimed that some online workers did not identify any specific circumstances that would see them leave sex work, rather they saw their engagement with sex work as more open-ended. For example, Helen was open to the idea of being able to come and go from sex work because of the relative ease of returning: "It's kind of one of those jobs that you can come back to even if you decide to leave" (Drucker & Nieri, 2018, p. 7). This idea was also shared by Angie: "It's not like it's gone forever. If I really wanna do it, I can. If I don't I won't … It's not like, 'Hey, I'm a lawyer, and I got fired, and I can never get that back'" (Drucker & Nieri, 2018, p. 7). As Drucker and Nieri (2018) highlight, for the workers in their study, many moved in and out of sex work and could do so without this impacting on things like health coverage, paid leave, employer contributions to pensions or superannuation, stock options etc., as sometimes these benefits are not formally provided in sex work.

This fluid relationship with sex work has been documented in studies in other sectors of the industry, including indoor and outdoor workers. For example, Sanders (2007) developed the idea of street and indoor sex workers 'yo-yoing', with a large portion of participants in her study describing how leaving sex work was preceded "by a period of moving in and out of sex work, taking breaks and struggling to decide what to do next" (2007, p. 88). Latisha, a street-based sex worker, spoke about having to return to sex work after receiving a fine for soliciting and having no other way to pay, while indoor workers discussed the psychological stress of the job meaning they had to take time out for their mental health, but return for the money (Sanders, 2007). In Cimino's (2019) study "easy money" was a factor brought up by multiple participants in relation to the decision to start and/or return to sex work. Serenity, a business owner and former street-based worker who had not sex worked for 10 years considered returning to support her daughter with buying books for college (Cimino, 2019, p. 612). Sierra, also a street-based worker, was supported financially by her brother to leave sex work, but viewed the job as something she could always fall back on (Cimino, 2019,

p. 612). Finally, Maher et al. (2012) discuss the value of flexible well-paid work for women working in indoor locations in Melbourne, Australia. For the workers in their study, who were also parents and students, the flexibility and conditions available in sex work were important in their decisions around moving into, out of and back into sex work. Their research showed how the good ratio between hours at work and income earned in scheduling were key benefits associated with sex work flexibility and women's fluid engagements with sex work (Maher et al., 2012). Sandy (2014) reported similar conditions for women workers in Cambodia's brothels, where sex work offered benefits and flexibility to women not available in other jobs.

In Gilmour's (2020) research with Melbourne-based sex workers, while sex work may have been undertaken in situations of desperation, their consideration of career trajectories illustrates how not all sex work was simply a means of survival. For example, Annika returned to sex work, and described her re-entry to Gilmour as follows:

> we had no furniture, we were sleeping on the floor in the middle of winter, we're all wearing four jumpers, my little baby daughter who I'd always sworn I'd get a better life for her – but we've got no bed, no mattress, we've got no pillows. ... I was going three and four days without food. I just thought ...: 'Hang on, I used to be a sex worker. I can still do that' (Gilmour, 2020, p. 301).

Annika's re-entry into sex work was a financial necessity; however, she stayed in sex work for 18 years, with the work allowing her to make long-term life choices: "I was able to put aside money and buy homes. And so for me to leave [the sex industry], it was easier because I had financial backing. I owned my own house" (Gilmour, 2020, p. 302). As Gilmour notes, Annika's re-entry reflected an absence of choice, but "her significant earning potential and flexible work hours were translated into tertiary study and multiple home ownership – a position from which she had options in how she chose to leave the industry (she had a professional career and was a published author at the time of interview)" (Gilmour, 2020, p. 302).

Sex work studies show how some workers keep the idea of sex working open as an option for future employment. For some, this fluidity may be because of the nature of the work, for others, they go back into sex work because they want to, while some may face limited choices, and here it is important to recognise how workers keep their options open. It is a way for workers to control how and when they leave sex work, and instead of being read as 'chaotic', what we can see here is how workers can and do demonstrate and exercise agency in setting their own agendas, timelines and relationships with sex work to align with their personal lives.

5.3.3 *Retirement Planning: Moving Beyond the Binary*

Sex workers' career planning shows how workers strategise their engagement with the industry and how long they plan to work in it to fulfil their diverse goals. These goals may be short-term or long-term, which can shape their working and retirement plans. For example, in Drucker and Nieri's study, Doris, an online worker, reflected on the circumstances in which she wanted to retire: "I really want to reach my goal ... and then have retirement ... and delete my profile" (2018, pp. 6–7). These sentiments were shared by some escort workers in Ham and Gilmour's (2016) study who spoke about developing an 'exit plan' or strategy that shaped sex work practices. When discussing how a sex worker's exit plan influenced approaches to sex work and work practices, Lily, a Melbourne-based Asian independent escort, explained this as:

> If you are [in it] for the money, you have to have very clear goals. You have to come up with a specific number of what you want to make. And from that number you can deduct how many bookings you would have to make. And how much time you can spare to be involved in it. You have to make the choice whether you do it on the side and it takes a little bit longer, or you actually just throw yourself in full-time and try to make as much money as you can in as short amount of time as you can (Ham & Gilmour, 2016, p. 7).

Lily's experiences differ from the dominant 'exiting' narratives we explored in Chapter 2. Her reflections show how workers can and do use retirement plans to strengthen work practices and success in sex work, regardless of whether they stay in or leave the industry. In Drucker and Nieri's (2018) study, some online workers had similar long-term career plans and retirement strategies. For example, Eva discussed retirement as being able to stop work because of meeting financial goals, which she compared against 'quitting' sex work without saving money or achieving goals: "I view retirement as after you got a really nice car, you have a stable home ... you can retire and not be on any type of site, and still text your regulars ... not like, I'm so over this. Going into retirement ... That's called quitting" (Drucker & Nieri, 2018, p. 7). Other online workers discussed a more phased approach to stepping out of sex work, like Crystal who "intended to 'just slowly like drift out ... not see new clients' and keep seeing 'regulars' as long as they adequately paid her", while Vicky planned to "become more exclusive: less posting, more regular people that I know, and more longer arrangements, rather than like hours and half hours" (Drucker & Nieri, 2018, p. 7).

In her study with indoor and outdoor workers in the UK, Sanders (2007) found that while some workers left the industry through a process of gradual planning, there were significant differences in and how they discussed and understood the process. For example, in Sanders' study, indoor workers like Clara tended to identify as career workers and spoke of retirement plans:

> to have a successful exit route you've got to have some other form of income coming in and you've got to have a very realistic approach to how much you need to live on; one of the major factors being the money side of it (Sanders, 2007, p. 84).

Clara's words resonate with Lily's featured above. Lily and Clara show how sex workers' 'exit plans' and strategies shape their approach to sex work and working practices. They also highlight the role of dual careers with sex work supplementing and supporting other careers or studies (see also Bowen (2021); Gilmour (2020); Law (2013) and Pickering et al. (2009)). For street-based sex workers, Sanders (2007, p. 84) noted how gradual planning might start with a methadone program or other holistic interventions designed to address multiple issues (e.g., addiction, abuse, exclusion), rehousing and/or reconciliation with family or children who had been placed in care. The process was more commonly associated with working closely with service providers in an intensive case management approach, as discussed by Zoe:

> [safe housing is] ... very important if you want to rehabilitate because you can't rehabilitate and live on the streets because its [drugs] all around you. If you take yourself away from the normal places you go to, although it's more isolated there's less temptation because you don't know anybody. And if you have got some kind of support, someone to come and see you

> fit in your appointments to get your medication and that type of thing you can overcome it (Sanders, 2007, p. 84).

These experiences highlight the need to work with different groups of sex workers in designing and developing appropriate conceptual frameworks, policy interventions and programs. In reviewing the literature on sex workers' experiences, we have documented some commonalities across work sectors, but also significant and notable differences, which suggest the need to consider different modalities. For example, an intensive case management approach might be appropriate for facilitating transitions for a worker like Zoe, but entirely inappropriate for Clara where a community health-based approach using peer learning might be more appropriate. The research shows that, while both Zoe and Clara may fit into the category of 'gradual planning', their needs are quite different. As the literature demonstrates, for most sex workers, leaving the industry was not a singular event nor was it a linear process, and it is one with varying degrees of complexity and factors informing workers' decision-making. While some workers see their involvement in sex work as temporary, others see this through a more long-term lens. For example, Ham and Gilmour highlight how escort workers planning a long-term career in the industry "employed a range of strategies including dual careers, contingency plans (e.g., further education, substantial savings) and an expected end date (e.g., at age 50)" (2016, p. 5). Sex workers' own personal timelines in the industry can and do differ, and some of the factors influencing this included motivations for work, personal and financial goals and intended end dates, which can impact on how and when they approach leaving sex work. As Ham and Gilmour argue, the challenge this poses in developing responses is the need to:

> reconcile the mobility that characterises sex work and the diversity of sex workers' motivations with a dominant exiting narrative in which an encompassing industry ensnares vulnerable women who require assistance in order to escape. Furthermore, the temporariness of the work for many people, alongside the considerable planning evident among [sex workers] and their legitimate concerns around de-skilling, all need to be considered in any exit programming (2016, p.13).

Clearly, any model attempting to address 'exiting' needs to consider how decision-making processes and career development planning differs by work location and intersecting factors like age, class, race, ethnicity, migration, gender, sex work laws and so on. It is vitally important that this model also addresses the main reasons for workers leaving sex work, which is crucial in understanding worker motivations and facilitating transitions while also enabling choice and autonomy. Again, this is, this is something that may also differ by work location.

5.4 Conclusion

This chapter has highlighted some of the benefits and challenges with formal 'exiting' programs through exploring sex workers' experiences engaging in 'exiting' provisions. 'Hitting bottom', going through a turning point event, and experiences with the police and violence were detailed as reasons for leaving the industry. This suggests the need for tailored support to help sex workers navigate this transition through therapy, drug and alcohol support, financial support, career upskilling or re-skilling and study. Religious organisations were useful in aiding some sex workers making sense of their lives and receiving love and compassion, while adopting 'mainstream identities'. However, there are some notable challenges here with using religion as a way to abstain from what is seen as 'bad' behaviour and where issues of morality tended to dominate in approaches, which can reinforce sex work stigma. As we argued in the previous chapter, pervasive sex work stigma and discrimination means that support might be needed in this area. Therefore, we need to be mindful about perpetrating stigma and discrimination and reinforcing ideas about sex work and sex workers as 'unworthy subjects' in 'exiting' programs.

In this chapter, we have shown that it is important conceptual frameworks do not assume sex workers are starting at 'ground zero' and have no knowledge or career planning skills. Clearly, this chapter demonstrates that this is not the case. In discussions about their work, sex workers show how sex work is skilled labour, and career planning was a key skill workers developed in navigating the sometimes-precarious nature of sex work and labour market dynamics. Indeed, as we have shown, and as Maher et al. (2012) and Sandy (2014) argue, the lack of flexibility and comparable pay in other industries are crucial in understanding worker decisions about starting, staying in and leaving sex work. As Maher et al. (2012) argue, the focus on criminalisation, harm and stigma in research, while necessary, can work to obscure an understanding of the importance of working conditions, flexibility and gendered labour market dynamics. This means our frameworks end up missing the centrality of this in workers' decision-making processes and career planning, which is also largely absent from policy and practice. In concluding, we need to move beyond the in/out binary and regulatory frameworks that favour deviance or criminalisation as this closes off on understanding the interplay between labour market conditions and dynamics and sex worker decision-making and agency. Building on the analyses undertaken in this chapter, the following chapter sets out a new framework for understanding transitions and 'exits' shaped around the idea of sex work careers and career development to open up possibilities for different realities, policies and programs and shift theoretical and policy debates.

References

Barry, K. (1995). *The prostitution of sexuality.* New York University Press.

Benoit, C., Jansson, S. M., Smith, M., & Flagg, J. (2018). Prostitution stigma and its effect on the working conditions, personal lives, and health of sex workers. *The Journal of Sex Research, 55*(4–5), 457–471. https://doi.org/10.1080/00224499.2017.1393652

Bindel, J., Brown, L., Easton, H., & Matthews, R., Reynolds Eaves, L., & London South Bank University. (2012). *Breaking down barriers: A study of how women exit prostitution.* Eaves, London South Bank University & Big Lottery Fund. Online: https://i4.cmsfiles.com/eaves/2012/11/Breaking-down-the-barriers-a37d80.pdf

Bishop, R., & Robinson, L. (1998). *Night market: Sexual cultures and the Thai economic miracle.* Routledge.

Bowen, R. (2015). Squaring up: Experiences of transition from off-street sex work to square work and duality – concurrent involvement in both – in Vancouver, BC. *Canadian Review of Sociology, 52*(4), 429–449. https://doi.org/10.1111/cars.12085

Bowen, R. (2021). *Work, money and duality: Trading sex as a side hustle.* Bristol University Press.

Brennan, D. (2004). *What's love got to do with it? Transnational desires and sex tourism in the Dominican Republic.* Duke University Press.

Brown, L. (2000). *Sex slaves: The trafficking of women in Asia.* Virago.

Busza, J. (2004). Sex work and migration: The dangers of oversimplification – A case study of Vietnamese women in Cambodia. *Health and Human Rights, 7*(2), 231–49. https://www.jstor.org/stable/4065357

Campbell, C. (2003). *"Letting them die": Why HIV/AIDS intervention programmes fail.* The International African Institute with Double Storey Books & Indiana University Press.

Chapkis, W. (1997). *Live sex acts: Women performing erotic labor.* Routledge.

Cimino, A. (2019). Uncovering intentions to exit prostitution: Findings from a qualitative study. *Victims & Offenders, 14*(5), 606–624. https://doi.org/10.1080/15564886.2019.1628144

Day, S. (2007). *On the game: Women and sex work.* Pluto Press.

Dalla, R. (2006). "You can't hustle all your life": An exploratory investigation of the exit process among street-level prostituted women. *Psychology of Women Quarterly, 30*, 276–290. https://doi.org/10.1111/j.1471-6402.2006.00296.x

Deer, S., Zarestky, J. & Baumgartner, L. (2021). 'Relive my life from scratch': Learning through transition for women exiting the sex trade. *Learning, Culture and Social Interaction, 29*(2021), 100501. https://doi.org/10.1016/j.lcsi.2021.100501

Derks, A. (2008). *Khmer women on the move: Migration and urban experiences in Cambodia.* University of Hawaii Press.

Drucker, J., & Nieri, T. (2018). Female online sex workers' perceptions of exit from sex work. *Deviant Behavior, 39*(1), 1–19. https://doi.org/10.1080/01639625.2016.1257890

Farley, M. (2007). *Prostitution and trafficking in Nevada: Making the connections.* Prostitution Research and Education.

Ford, M., & Lyons, L. (2011). Narratives of agency: Sex work in Indonesia's borderlands. In K. Adams & K. Gillogly (Eds.), *Everyday life in Southeast Asia* (pp. 295–303). Indiana University Press.

Gesser, N., & Shdaimah, C. (2021). "I'm doing everything right all over again": How women manage exiting street prostitution over time. *Journal of Qualitative Criminal Justice & Criminology, 10*(4), Article 3. https://dc.swosu.edu/qc/vol10/iss4/3

Gilmour, F. (2020). Careers in the Australian sex industry: Exploring life narratives through metaphor. *Journal of Sociology, 56*(3), 297–313. https://doi.org/10.1177/1440783319893462

Groves, J., Newton, D., Chen, M., Hocking, J., Bradshaw, C., & Fairley, C. (2008). Sex workers working within a legalised industry: Their side of the story. *Sexually Transmitted Infections, 84*(5), 393–394. https://doi.org/10.1136/sti.2008.030668

Ham, J., & Gilmour, F. (2016). 'We all have one': Exit plans as a professional strategy in sex work. *Work, Employment and Society, 31*(5), 748–763. https://doi.org/10.1177/0950017016666198

Hedin, U., & Månsson, S. (2004). The importance of supportive relationships among women leaving prostitution. *Journal of Trauma Practice, 2*(3–4), 223–237. https://doi.org/10.1300/J189v02n03_13

Kempadoo, K. (1999). The migrant tightrope: Experiences from the Caribbean. In K. Kempadoo & J. Doezema (Eds.), *Global sex workers: Rights, resistance, and redefinition* (pp. 124–138). Routledge.

Kulick, D. (1998). *Travesti: Sex, gender, and culture among Brazilian transgendered prostitutes*. University of Chicago Press.

Law, L. (2000). *Sex work in Southeast Asia: The place of desire in a time of AIDS*. Routledge.

Law, T. (2013). Transitioning out of sex work: Exploring sex workers' experiences and perspectives. In E. van der Meulen, E. Durisin, & V. Love (Eds.), *Selling sex: Experience, advocacy, and research on sex work in Canada* (pp. 101–110). UBC Press.

Lim, L., & International Labour Office. (1998). *The sex sector: The economic and social bases of prostitution in Southeast Asia*. International Labour Office.

Maher, J., Pickering, S., & Gerard, A. (2012). Privileging work not sex: Flexibility and employment in the sexual services industry. *The Sociological Review, 60*, 546–675. https://doi.org/10.1111/j.1467-954X.2012.02128.x

Månsson, S., & Hedin, U. (1999). Breaking the Matthew effect - on women leaving prostitution. *International Journal of Social Welfare, 8*, 67–77. https://doi.org/10.1111/1468-2397.00063

Matthews, D. (2024). *An exploration of how sex workers who identify as religious or spiritual manage their identities within their everyday lives* [Doctoral dissertation, Nottingham Trent University]. https://irep.ntu.ac.uk/id/eprint/51091/

Mayhew, P., & Mossman, E. (2007). *Exiting prostitution: Models of best practice*. Victoria University of Wellington. Online: https://www.nzpc.org.nz/pdfs/Mayhew-and-Mossman,-(2007c)-Exiting-Prostitution-Models-of-best-practice.pdf

Murray, A. (2001). *Pink fits: Sex, subcultures and discourses in the Asia-Pacific*. Monash Asia Institute.

Norma, C., & Tankard-Reist, M. (2016). *Prostitution narratives: Stories of survival in the sex trade*. Spinifex.

Oselin, S. (2010). Weighing the consequences of a deviant career: Factors leading to an exit from prostitution. *Sociological Perspectives, 53*(4), 527–549. https://doi.org/10.1525/sop.2010.53.4.527

Parreñas, R. (2011). *Illicit flirtations: Labor, migration and sex trafficking in Tokyo*. Stanford University Press.

Pickering, S., Maher, J., & Gerard, A. (2009). *Working in Victorian brothels: An independent report commissioned by Consumer Affairs Victoria into the Victorian brothel sector*. Monash University.

Puffer, H., Hodson, G., & Prusaczyk, E. (2024). Attitudes toward cisgender women's participation in sex work: Opportunity for agency or harmful exchange? *Archives of Sexual Behaviour, 53*, 1169–1185. https://doi.org/10.1007/s10508-023-02797-y

Sanders, T. (2005). *Sex work: A risky business*. Willan.

Sanders, T. (2007). Becoming an ex-sex worker: Making transitions out of a deviant career. *Feminist Criminology, 2*(1), 74–95. https://doi.org/10.1177/1557085106294845

Sandy, L. (2014). *Women and sex work in Cambodia: Blood, sweat and tears*. Routledge.

Toubiana, M., & Ruebottom, T. (2022). Stigma hierarchies: The internal dynamics of stigmatization in the sex work occupation. *Administrative Science Quarterly, 67*(2), 515–552. https://doi.org/10.1177/00018392221075344

Wardlow, H. (2006). *Wayward women: Sexuality and agency in a New Guinea society*. University of California Press.

Williamson, C., & Folaron, G. (2003). Understanding the experiences of street level prostitutes. *Qualitative Social Work, 2*(3), 271–287. https://doi.org/10.1177/14733250030023004

Wojcicki, J. (2002). "She drank his money": Survival sex and the problem of violence in taverns in Gauteng Province, South Africa. *Medical Anthropology Quarterly, 16*(3), 267–293. https://doi.org/10.1525/maq.2002.16.3.267

CHAPTER 6

Careers in Sex Work: Exploring 'Exiting' through the Lens of Career Development

Abstract This chapter reconceptualises 'exiting' as career development. Developed through the interface between Chapters 2 and 3 and building on our key arguments in Chapters 4 and 5, this chapter applies a career framing using case studies, interview data and secondary sources to demonstrate how the idea of career development rather than 'exiting', allows us to consider the ways in which these programs can align with traditional career transitioning and development programs. Career development programs focus on assisting a person's entry into a new occupation and skills development for supporting progression within a chosen profession or skills transfer and training for moving into a different field. In this chapter, we shift from debates about regulation and the focus on gendered inequalities related to heterosexuality (tied to morality politics), to sex work as career, and thus as work (tied to social inequalities and labour market dynamics). This chapter is a provocation to reconceptualise 'exiting' as career development, and in it we argue this is necessary if sex work is more clearly reconfigured within a career framework. Ultimately, this new framework allows us to recognise the socio-economic, political and cultural forces shaping career choices, while simultaneously challenging the deviance and victimhood framings that dominate discourse and policy in this area. Alongside this, we argue for the need to explore the role of stigma and criminalisation in shaping the ongoing need for these services and developing a grounded model for understanding what

L. Sandy et al., *Reconceptualizing Exiting and Career Development in Sex Work*, Palgrave Advances in Sex Work Studies,
https://doi.org/10.1007/978-3-032-10077-1_6

'exiting' might look like when sex work is recognised as a valid career choice.

Keywords Sex work · Career development · Sex work careers · Transitions · Sex worker inclusion · Vocational support · Flexible employment · Job precarity · Decriminalisation · Agency · Theory

6.1 Introduction

In this chapter, we use the idea of 'career' to challenge the highly individualised framings of personal choice' influencing sex work research and 'exiting' studies. So far, we have highlighted the consequences of this framing and here we extend our argument by sharing more results of our program analysis exploring best practice' in service provision, this time looking at examples from Australia and the UK. Again, like Chapter 3, we use a case study design to present two case studies describing and exploring programs in this area with examples drawn from our global program review. The case studies presented in this chapter use a particular framing that links with and furthers understanding sex work as work. The conceptual framework for the programs considered in this chapter were based on an understanding and appreciation of sex work as work and an occupation. This means sex work was defined as labour, and as we highlighted in Chapters 2 and 3, this was not the case in most 'exiting' programs. Typically, 'exiting' programs defined sex work as a form of harm or violence against women. By shifting the framing into work and occupation, these programs encourage us to start thinking about career development in sex work, which also challenges the in/out binary shaping 'exiting' programs. It also changes the focus, as much of the existing literature on 'exiting' sex work was concerned with the process of how the sex industry was left and new identities formed. This fixation on leaving the sex industry casts sex work as a social problem and people's involvement in it as a 'last resort', which 'exiting' interventions then address. Given this framing, as we showed in Chapter 2, a stages of change or role-exit logic is deemed appropriate, as it is seen as enabling researchers to identify where sex workers are at in their 'exiting' journey, but this means focus remains on understanding individual choices and actions, with the social and structural factors shaping life circumstances mainly used to explain why people start working in the industry (seen as a problem).

In this chapter, we show how the idea of career development can address workers' diverse needs and experiences, while also highlighting the non-linear processes through which people stop sex working. It fosters an understanding of the diverse working and employment practices in the sector and encourages us to see sex work as something a person does not have to be 'in' or 'out' of. Another key element of the argument we present in this chapter is that a career frame allows us to consider social contexts, gendered employment conditions and labour market dynamics. We use the concept to move beyond a singular focus on 'exiting' sex work and seeing this as a problem to facilitate a shift towards exploring how people can be supported when starting sex work as a new occupation or upskilling as part of career progression and sex working alongside other forms of work or studies. Here, we argue that this brings 'exiting' programs and services in line with career programming in other sectors where the focus is not about getting people out of a particular industry, but in developing professional skills, knowledges and experiences to achieve career goals. This idea was first stimulated when reflecting on interview data presented in Chapter 4, recall, "we don't exit judges" (Interview with Michael), "I've never been asked about exiting factory work or other jobs that I've done" (Interview with Ahi Wi-Hongi, NZPC) and Lexxie Jury's insightful comments:

> ...there's no other job in the world what has an exiting or transitioning position. I don't ever—as a SWOP outreach worker, no one's offering me a transitioning job, no one's offering me an exiting job. As a bank teller, as a cop, as a lawyer, as anything, nobody else is offered that. You get offered upskilling ... It's only as a sex worker that we're going to offer you a transitioning or an exiting program (Interview with Lexxie Jury, SWOP ACT).

Sex work is the only job where a person is offered 'help' to stop work. Lexxie Jury, Ahi Wi-Hongi and Michael are correct here, we don't offer 'exit' programs to other workers, which makes these programs discriminatory. This point was noted by Jane Green:

> I think one thing that's important to remember is, it's inherently discriminatory to think that we need exiting services ... when you're making an

> assumption about what sex workers need, I always tell people: take away the word sex worker and put plumber. If it sounds stupid, then you're probably doing something that's inherently discriminatory and stigmatising (Interview with Jane Green, Vixen Collective).

Jane Green is correct, we don't have 'exit' programs for plumbers, and frankly, it is an idea that sounds absurd. However, if say a judge wants to leave the profession, they can access retraining and re-skilling alongside skills training and professional development activities through standard career development programs offered to most workers—a point made by Lexxie Jury. This leads us to argue for a career development framing as tackling some of key issues with 'exiting' programs raised in Chapters 4 and 5, while permitting an exploration of major themes in the career development literature, which include: theoretical perspectives on careers, the social context of careers (workplaces, intersectionality (race, ethnicity, class, gender, age, sexuality, abilities etc.), organisational environments, work-life interface, gendered employment structures), career evolution and development, career decision-making, variations in careers, career development initiatives, job searching and recruitment and professional associations (Greenhaus & Callanan, 2006). The idea of career development refocuses our attention to worker mobility and upskilling within the industry and supporting people when they start sex work or maintain dual careers, while also addressing the needs of workers who want to leave the industry. Ultimately, it is a framing that recognises complexity and expands life choices, while supporting a person's right to determine whether they want to stay in or leave sex work.

This chapter, then, links the issues explored in other chapters to *work* and not sex, because as Maher et al. (2012) argue, debates about regulation focus on gendered inequalities related to heterosexuality, and thus remain wedded to morality politics, more than they recognise social inequalities related to labour market conditions. Ultimately, while the focus on criminalisation, harm, stigma and exploitation may be necessary, as we showed in our previous chapter, this often comes at the expense of, or obscures an understanding of sex workers' decision-making and individual and collective agency. In expanding our argument, we argue that a more direct focus on employment contexts and careers in sex work is needed to produce grounded research, policy and programs in this area.

6.2 Careers in Sex Work

The prevailing view of sex work as deviant behaviour means many people think it is wrong, or alternatively, as a form of violence and exploitation, sex workers are victims. This means that sex work is often said to be something no one would ever choose to do (i.e., sex work as a 'last resort'). However, in Chapter 5, we showed how sex workers can and do make decisions about sex work based on other work options available to them, and deciding on career pathways, or ways of engaging in sex work. The idea of sex work careers involves individual career planning, but caution needs to be exercised that ideas about personal choice do not once again dominate discussion as is often the case with sex work research. The concept of career is important here as it allows exploration of career patterns and trends from which we can shift between the micro, meso and macro levels of analysis. If we look at the idea of career trajectories, sex work involves short-, medium- and long-term goal setting and career planning, but what this looks like will differ and can be shaped by a person's motivation for doing sex work as we showed in Chapter 5. These reasons are often influenced by the broader gendered labour market and social inequalities that are shaped by intersecting structures (e.g., a person's race, gender, sexuality, abilities etc.) (Benoit & Mellor, 2023; Bowen, 2021; Gilmour, 2020; Sandy, 2014).

Long-term planning can involve things like upskilling in sex work, mobility within sex work, further studies and dual careers in sex work and 'straight' or 'square' work. Mid-to long-term career planning might look like sex work as a primary career or as part of a parallel career trajectory (Bowen, 2021; Gilmour, 2020). Sex work career planning might also involve sex working alongside study, property investment and 'straight' work (Gilmour, 2020). As an example of sex work careers, one participant in Gilmour's study, Vivian was:

> undertaking postgraduate study in her 'straight' career, had a certificate in brothel management, extensive reception experience, trained in BDSM, invested in dungeon furniture and fetish material, and had developed a private client base as well as her brothel work. She was well placed both to continue a career in the sex industry, and to pursue her straight career and she intended to do both (2020, p. 305).

Vivian's approach to sex work was long-term and goal-oriented while also being fluid, allowing her to undertake university studies while sex working. Understanding Vivian's sex work as career allows us to recognise sex work *is* skilled labour. Vivian highlights how sex workers have experience in a variety of jobs with diverse skills and experiences, which is contrary to the framing of sex work as a dead-end job and sex workers as needing "some massive amount of help to do something else ... or that sex work is not skilled work, and we have no skills" (Interview with Jane Green, Vixen Collective). In addition to viewing sex work as skilled work, sex work as career allows us to recognise that many sex workers have experience in 'straight' jobs with different skills that can assist in making career changes, whether that be starting or leaving sex work, or more moving around sectors or different roles in the industry.

Unlike Vivian's more longer-term engagement, sex work can be temporary and short-term. Sex work as career allows us to recognise how people's engagement in sex work can be for shorter periods and often goal oriented. As Gilmour (2020) notes, for some Melbourne-based sex workers, short-term engagement in sex work enabled specific life transitions like making the transition to single parenting, for others it was to support studies. Sandy (2014) documented short-term engagement in sex work by some Cambodian sex workers to meet the challenges of the precarious financial situation women found themselves in, or to pay for medical bills and treatment or for others to save to buy a house or land. These reasons will shape a person's engagement in sex work and sex work as career can be a way to manage economic precarity and social inequalities. Sex work provides flexible and temporary work, and this was recognised as one of the advantages of the work; however, career allows recognition that workers do need to protect against this with forward planning, while also working to enhance sex workers' safety and health (Gilmour, 2020).

Sex work as career helps us understand how leaving sex work becomes part of a person's expected career and employment trajectory. This might be more gradual, and part of a natural progression, while for others this may be more short-term and deliberate. Career also recognises that some workers, like Vivian, plan their careers within the industry and have no desire to leave, while other sex workers may upskill and transition within the industry to other roles. As Gilmour argues:

> rather than seeing the sex industry as a dead-end job, it is therefore more accurate to understand it as a career with job opportunities, which are nonetheless structured by temporal aspects – the retrogressive [policy]

dynamic, the shape of women's career trajectories and family lives, and the flexibility of the work itself (which allows women to intertwine it with their mothering activities and education goals so successfully) (2020, p. 306-7).

The idea of sex work as career shows that we need to exercise caution with 'rescue' approaches and framings that view sex workers as victims. In Chapter 5, we showed how many sex workers carefully planned their time and involvement in sex work. They also carefully planned and managed transitions within and out of sex work. This means that "exiting [does] not stand in opposition to sex work", as the in/out binary suggests (Gilmour, 2020, p. 307). As Ham and Gilmour argue, sex work and 'exiting' can be "symbiotic, with exit plans shaping a strategic and focused approach to sex work, and sex work enabling transitions into other areas" (2016, p. 761).

However, research also shows that this can be a complicated process for some sex workers. Sex work as career allows us to understand how leaving sex work can be hard for some people. For example, Blake found it hard to leave sex work, despite repeated attempts to do so: "push comes to shove and you get a whole heap of bills, well you can't pay them, what are you going to do? You're going to end up homeless or you're going to go back to what you know" (Gilmour, 2020, p. 307). In Gilmour's (2020) study, Blake spoke about the "pretty amazing" support she had received in an 'exit' program, but had not been able to make the transition into 'straight' work (Gilmour, 2020, p. 307). This is because of the downward mobility that often comes with minimum wage work offered to sex workers by 'exit' programs, which another sex worker, Christine described as an "absolute fucking failure" (Gilmour, 2020, p. 307). Understanding sex work as career highlights how 'exit' programs can fail to meet the needs and interests of all sex workers. Chan Dyna from the Cambodian Prostitutes Union explains:

> I do not want to go to your shelter and learn to sew so you can get me to work in a factory. This is not what I want. If I tell you that you will call me a *srei coit* [*srey kouc* whore/prostitute]. But those words are easy for you because you have easy solutions to difficult problems you do not understand, and you do not understand because you do not listen (Chan, 1999, p. 179).

'Exiting' programs are premised on the idea that providing alternatives can end exploitation in sex work. This logic is faulty on a few different levels. Firstly, the focus on sex work abolition it means that exploitation and abuses in the industry are not addressed. Secondly, it promotes means that exploitation, abuses and working conditions in other labour sectors that factor into people's decisions to start sex work are rarely considered (Sandy, 2014). As Gilmour argues, "the same labour market forces that help shape entry into the industry (poor work conditions, particularly in low-skilled feminized work, and a dearth of flexible employment) can also limit options for successfully transitioning out of the industry" (2020, p. 307). This was poignantly noted by Alice, a Scottish sex worker interviewed by the BBC about recent efforts to introduce the Swedish Model and 'exiting' programs in Scotland. Alice said that an 'exiting' program "doesn't really change why some people end up choosing to do sex work in the first place" (Wallace Lockhart, 2025, n.p.). Finally, this leads us to the ultimate paradox in 'exiting':

> It is easy to say that alternative work should be made available to women working in prostitution but harder to say exactly how this could be done (and incomes maintained) or even why it should be done (especially if sex work is not seen to have a universal/essentialist meaning and if women are seen to have at least some agentic capacity as workers in a globalized world economy) (Sullivan, 2003, p. 78).

Sex work as career presents a nuanced and complex picture of people's working lives and trajectories into, within and out of sex work. Using this framework, we can see how people make complex, multifaceted decisions about their lives and careers, and how these decisions are influenced by socio-economic conditions, gendered labour markets and social positions shaped by intersecting structures (e.g., race, gender, age, sexuality, disability etc.). In the following section, we explore what a career development program looks like in two different legislative settings, partial criminalisation and legalisation.

6.3 From 'Exiting' to Career Development: Sex Worker-Led Programs

'Exiting' programs developed by sex workers and for sex workers have a very different approach to transitions. In this section, we present evidence from our global program review where we found pockets of promising practice in this area of service provision under two different legislative frameworks, namely legalisation (Queensland, Australia) and partial criminalisation (the United Kingdom). In what follows, we describe two career development programs offered by sex worker organisations to highlight the different approaches taken to program development and services offered. We draw out the importance of embedding lived experience expertise in program design and reflect on advances in sex industry policy and programs where sex workers are included as experts and not objects.

6.3.1 Career Development under Legalisation

We begin our discussion with a career development program developed in Queensland, Australia. Sex work laws are different in each state and territory in Australia, and because of this, we will explain the range of regulatory regimes in place to clear up some of the confusion about sex work laws in that country, after which we present our case study.

Australia is unique in that almost every regulatory regime is in place in the states and territories, apart from sex purchase laws (i.e., the Swedish Model). Starting in the Australian Capital Territory (ACT), sex work was legalised under the *Sex Work Act* (1992). The ACT government operates a licensing system with mandatory condom use. Street-based sex work is criminalised along with cooperative working arrangements (several independent workers working together with no management) (Scarlet Alliance, 2024). There have been multiple attempts to decriminalise sex work in South Australia, all of which have been unsuccessful. Sex work decriminalisation has been debated in this state since the 1980s, with several private members bills put forward, but these have been defeated (the last private members bill was defeated by a very narrow margin in 2019). As Baratosy and Wendt argue, in South Australia, "reform of the sex industry remains stagnant and hence sex work remains criminalized" (2017, p. 34). This means that South Australia has the oldest and most punitive laws in the country. The laws are confusing and inconsistently applied which works to create a climate of fear for sex workers and makes it very difficult to for them to work safely (Baratosy & Wendt, 2017; Scarlet Alliance, 2024). Sex work was criminalised under the *Summary Offences Act* (1953). In the state, sex businesses (brothels and massage and escort agencies), independent sex work and street-based sex work are criminalised (Scarlet Alliance, 2024). Tasmania operates a framework of partial criminalisation. Under the Sex Industry Offences Act (2005) 'sexual service businesses' involving one or two self-employed workers working together are legal. Businesses with a 'commercial operator' managing sex workers are considered 'commercial sexual services businesses' and are criminalised. Street-based sex work is also criminalised (workers and clients) (Scarlet Alliance, 2024). Western Australia also operates a system of partial criminalisation, as while sex work is legal, most of the activities associated with it are illegal. Independent work is legal as is brothel and escort agency-based work. However, it is illegal to operate a brothel or escort agency, unless approved by the police (McKewon, 2005; Sandy, 2000). Street-based sex work is also illegal (Scarlet Alliance, 2024).

Moving to New South Wales, sex work was decriminalised in the late 1970s, making it the first jurisdiction in the world to decriminalise sex work. Decriminalisation was more a process, starting with the removal of penalties for street-based sex work in 1979 and the decriminalisation of brothels in 1995 (Aroney & Crofts, 2019). Most sex work was decriminalised in the state, but it stopped short of full decriminalisation. Sex work is regulated by local council planning laws and regulations and workplace health and safety and public health laws. Street-based sex work is restricted to certain areas (Scarlet Alliance, 2024). The *Sex Industry Act* (2019) decriminalised sex work in the Northern Territory. Sex businesses are subjected to planning requirements and are regulated by WorkSafe Northern Territory. Business owners must have a 'suitability certificate' if they employ three or more workers and outdoor sex work is decriminalised (Scarlet Alliance, 2024). We discuss the previous legislation in place in Queensland in our case study below as in May 2024, the government of that state passed the *Criminal Code (Decriminalising Sex Work) and Other Legislation Amendment Bill*, which came into effect on 2 August 2024 (Scarlet Alliance, 2024). Local government rules apply to all businesses and independent workers, who can also work together and employ support staff. Street-based sex work is decriminalised (workers and clients) (Scarlet Alliance, 2024). Sex work in Victoria was decriminalised under the *Sex Work Decriminalisation Act* (2022). Sex businesses and independent workers are regulated under local government planning laws and by WorkSafe Victoria. Street-based sex work is not fully decriminalised as it is restricted to certain areas and times (Scarlet Alliance, 2024).

Australia is an interesting microcosm for the range of legislative frameworks in place, but also the approach taken with recent legislative change towards decriminalisation. Sex worker activists have played leading roles in laying the foundations for decriminalisation across the country, but as we can see, roadblocks remain. In Australia, there has been a long history of sex worker activists contributing to law reforms, kickstarted by the Australian Prostitutes Collective who submitted groundbreaking research to the Select Committee of the New South Wales Legislative Assembly on Prostitution (1983–1986), which informed the ongoing decriminalisation of sex work in the state (Aroney & Crofts, 2019). This was followed by the Prostitutes Collective of Victoria making a submission calling for sex work decriminalisation to the Neave Inquiry in 1985, which started the long journey to decriminalisation in that Australian state (Overs, 2020). Australia is also unique in that it is a country where, in most states and territories, sex workers have been meaningfully included in law reform processes. Across the world, sex work law reform is often undertaken without the input of those most affected by the policies, namely sex workers, and as we have shown, this has mostly resulted in moralistic policy designed to protect or punish women (Aroney & Crofts, 2019; Garofalo Geymonat & Macioti, 2016; Wagenaar & Altink, 2012). The work of the Australian Prostitutes Collective and Prostitutes Collective of Victoria disrupted and challenged the construction of sex workers as 'victims' or 'deviants' and argued for their inclusion in the policymaking process. In Australia, other sex worker organisations and programs like Scarlet Alliance (including the Lutruwita (Tasmanian) sex worker project), Respect Inc (Queensland), the Vixen Collective (Victoria), RhED (Victoria), SWOP NSW (New South Wales), SWOP NT (Northern Territory), SWOP ACT (Australian Capital Territory), Magenta (Western Australia), SWEAR WA (Western Australia) and SIN (South Australia) have continued with this groundbreaking work. As Aroney and Crofts argue "the involvement of sex worker organisations in 'authentic dialogue' with government fosters an escape from the 'ideology driven' approaches" common in sex work laws (2019, p. 52). For Aroney and Crofts, key to legislative change in Australia was Wagenaar's (2017) idea of 'authentic dialogue' as:

> it emphasises more than simply telling sex workers what is good for them or allowing them to express their views. It *listens* to sex workers' critiques and recommended legal and regulatory approaches and includes them in policy formation (2019, p. 52).

These are important advances in sex industry policymaking where sex workers were included in policy formation as experts in the field rather than objects (Aroney & Crofts, 2019). It shows a way forward in a policy field that is often stagnant and ideologically driven. In Australia, the use of evidence informed by sex workers' lived experiences has worked to create a policy shift away from moralistic discourse and framings to practical and realistic policy formation focused on improving worker safety and conditions.

Before decriminalisation, sex work was legalised in Queensland under the Prostitution Act (1999). Sex work was legal in licensed brothels and condom use was mandatory. Street-based sex work was criminalised, as were outcalls from a brothel. Independent work was legal, but cooperative working arrangements were not. An independent worker could employ security and/or a driver, but the person had to have a valid crowd controller's license, and very strict laws applied to advertising (Sandy et al., 2019). Like the state of Victoria that also ran a licensing system under legalisation prior to decriminalisation in 2022, this essentially resulted in a two-tier system made up of a heavily regulated 'legal' sector, with the rest of the industry unlicensed and criminalised (Pickering et al., 2009; Rowe, 2011). In the following case study, we explore a career development program developed under legalisation in the Australian state of Queensland. In our case study, we propose that sex worker organisations like Respect Inc, who work to empower sex workers and fight for their rights, have played an instrumental role in legal reform and addressing sex work stigma as well as reconceptualising 'exiting' as career development.

Career Development Program, Respect Inc, Queensland, Australia

Background Queensland has a long history of offering 'exiting' programs for sex workers. Re-training/'exiting' programs were introduced with legalisation under the *Prostitution Act (1999)* (Crime & Misconduct Commission (CMC), 2004). Respect Inc is a peer-based organisation run by current and past sex workers to provide community development and health promotion to Queensland sex workers (Respect Inc, 2021). Prior to Respect Inc receiving funding for the career development program, the 'exiting' program offered by the state government was run by a variety of agencies. The last agency to offer the program, BSI Learning, delivered a service that adopted a case management approach similar to their post-release prison program (BSI Learning, 2013 a, b, c; CMC, 2011, p. 37). In 2016, Respect Inc developed the *Career Development Program* (CDP) with funding from the Queensland Government Department of Health. In developing the program, Respect Inc decided to run it as a career development program rather than an 'exiting' type of program. This is because:

> ... a lot of sex workers were saying that they felt that it would be better to run it in more of a development program rather than an exiting program and also to do it within a sex workers' rights framework rather than a—you know, because BSI were also running the post release prisoners' program, and they were doing the transitioning program with the post release prisoners' program ... [and that] didn't go down very well ... so there was a big push at the time that ... we would have a go ... so that it would be run with sex workers' empowerment [framework] (Interview with Respect Inc).

The Program After conducting a needs assessment with sex workers, Respect Inc designed a program that focused on career development rather than 'exiting'. The program focused on upskilling in sex work, with the activities designed to build upon and expand sex work and business skills alongside skills development for work outside of the industry. The program was tailored around providing services for sex workers who wanted to develop their careers inside and outside of sex work. Activities included basic bookkeeping skills, financial training (including tax returns and budgeting) as well as advertising, promotions and marketing. Other activities focused on building skills in growth areas in sex work, for example, Touching Base (skills training for providing services for people with disabilities) and other areas of specialised services (e.g., BDSM). Intensive case management was provided for workers with more complex needs (e.g., housing, mental health and/or alcohol and drug treatment).

CDP had two formats: a shorter three-month program or a longer twelve-month program for workers with more complex needs. The three-month program provided more of an information and referral service and the twelve-month program was focused on intensive case management, with program options shaped around the idea of starting in, moving within and out of sex work. The twelve-month program also came with access to a subsidy (max. value AU$800) provided by the Prostitution Licensing Authority. This worked to enable transitions by providing workers with assistance in meeting some of the costs associated with courses (for example, if a worker was not eligible for a Certificate III guarantee), or course materials and equipment (e.g., books or a laptop).

Respect Inc offered one-off skills building sessions on:

- Working differently in sex work
- Finding work in a different industry
- Job hunting
- Applications and résumé writing
- Tech and computer skills
- Education or course applications.

They also offered a case management program over 12-months, supporting sex workers to:

- Set goals
- Recognise and grow skills
- Develop skills in new areas
- Communicate their value to others
- Have confidence in their career progression
- Receive support from a diverse group of sex work peers (Respect Inc, 2023).

Our analysis of this case study shows that Respect Inc's *Career Development Program* meets the promising practice criteria that guided our global program review in a variety of ways. Firstly, the program was designed and developed through a community needs assessment, which ensured it met needs identified by sex workers. Secondly, the program model placed sex workers at the centre, applied the Ottawa Charter (WHO, 1986) and the key principle that the involvement of sex workers, as an affected community, was vital to sustainable and effective programs. This peer-led program was designed and developed by sex workers and based on a needs assessment, it was a program where the focus was not on 'exiting', but building and strengthening skills, increasing confidence and expanding life choices. It offered a holistic service provision where leaving sex work was one of the services and options available wherein the program goal was to support sex workers in making informed decisions. This means that 'exiting' was not the main goal, instead it was creating and enabling choices. The development and running of the program saw Respect Inc work very closely with Queensland Health to promote the benefits of the approach as compared with previous 'exiting' programs offered as part of post-prison services (and thus adopting a carceral framing and approach)—we can see some of the benefits of this approach filtering through in attitudinal and legislative change. The program developed by Respect Inc engaged with meaningful involvement and did not ascribe a victim status to sex workers, it offered holistic support to sex workers to help them achieve their career goals. In the following case study, we explore a similar program developed by a sex worker support organisation under partial criminalisation in the UK.

6.3.2 Career Development under Partial Criminalisation

In the UK, apart from Northern Ireland, sex work is partially criminalised, meaning that selling or buying sex is legal; however, a number of sex work practices are criminalised. This includes the organisation of sex work, keeping, managing, or assisting in the management of a brothel, involvement of a third party and soliciting (Platt et al., 2018). This means that it can be difficult for sex workers to work within legal frameworks safely (Sandy & Matthews, 2025). Under partial criminalisation, sex workers and the sex industry are seen as a social and legal problem that need to be controlled, with sex work framed as deviant behaviour. There are a number of 'exiting' programs within the UK that attempt to support sex workers to leave the industry, but the main aim of most programs was to reduce criminality, understood as selling sex (Hester & Westmarland, 2004). In this landscape of criminalisation and deviance, National Ugly Mugs (NUM) vocational support offers an alternative framing to the 'exiting' mindset, and instead, adopts the ethos of career development. NUM state, "our mission is to provide essential support and resources to sex workers, regardless of their choices about staying in or leaving the industry" (NUM, 2025, n.p.). We explore NUM's career development program below and show how, like our Queensland case study, vocation services that adopt promising practice can challenge the personal choice frameworks shaping 'exiting' programs and instead, offer services mirroring traditional career development programs alongside support for sex workers to overcome barriers to accessing alternative career options because of stigma.

Work! Work! Work!: Vocational Support Program, National Ugly Mugs, United Kingdom

Background NUM is a UK-wide charity working with sex workers to do research, design and deliver safety tools and provide services to people in adult industries (NUM, 2025). NUM offer an informal reporting system to keep sex workers safe, which allows sex workers to report incidents related to clients, that are then shared with other sex workers. Sex workers can also use this service to check clients' details and see if there have been reports made against them. This community-based reporting system stems from a program first developed by the Prostitutes Collective of Victoria in May 1986, known as Ugly Mugs (in Australian slang, a 'dodgy punter' or risky client is known as an ugly mug).

In 2022, NUM launched the Vocation, Vocation, Vocation project, which co-developed tools with sex workers to help improve their access to justice and support them to make informed decisions around their work (NUM, 2025). Following this, their vocational support services were then developed from two research projects. The first project, called *Leaving the Game*, saw NUM and the English Collective of Prostitutes document sex workers' career aspirations as well as the barriers to leaving sex work. This project explored how life circumstances, policies and national living costs have had a major impact on the decisions that individuals make and carried out a needs assessment to ensure support services were based on sex workers' needs (NUM, 2022; SWAN, 2019). After this, the *Changing the Game* project mapped support services for sex workers looking to make career changes (NUM, 2025). Through these key studies, NUM's vocational services were informed by research co-designed by sex workers, for sex workers.

The Program The *Work! Work! Work!* Program offered a range of online vocational support workshops, allowing sex workers to explore career options. For example, the *Changing the Game* workshop explored sex workers' career values, motivations and goals, with the remaining workshops focusing on key competencies and transferable skills, CV development and journey planning. NUM also offered an accelerated learning course developed for workers who feel more confident in their career planning (essentially the accelerated package combines the three workshops into one). When a sex worker completed the three workshops, they received access to one-to-one vocational support casework to support them with their career goals and signposting to additional financial support.

Alongside these workshops and case work, NUM also provided workspace vocational support hangouts (online and face-to-face), allowing sex workers to connect with their peers and share experiences, access mental health support, take part in skill share sessions, meet expert speakers in the field and provide well-being activities. The NUM project included a range of work-related online resources designed to support sex workers independently explore career options at their own pace. Sex workers accessed resources in any order and on topics applicable to them, as well as using these as a refresher tool. Within this service, NUM created downloadable workbooks to accompany each video (NUM, 2025).

Our analysis of this case study reveals that NUM created and delivered a peer-driven program, informed by sex workers to offer non-judgmental, tailored support. It adopted a rights-based approach to empower the community, meaning vocational support was not focused on 'exiting' sex work but offered holistic support around career aspirations within and outside of the industry. NUM's approach saw sex work as work and carried no precondition of workers having to leave the industry, instead the program offered services similar to career development programs outside of the sex industry, while recognising the barriers faced by sex workers due to stigma when changing their career. Respect Inc and NUM's vocation services highlight the potential for career development programs to adopt a promising practice framework, and over time, the ability to build this into best practice frameworks. While NUM's work illustrates the possibilities of career development through their services, it is important to acknowledge wider societal and legal challenges which exist under criminalising legislation and sex-negative environments that continue to downplay the importance of sex workers lived experience and expertise. The example of Respect Inc demonstrates what is possible when governments provide adequate funding to sex worker organisations and recognise their expertise in service design and delivery and developing policy and programs. It remains to be said that this does not necessarily mean that sex workers are seen as equal partners in dialogue as sex workers and sex worker advocates are often marginalised in Australian public discourse (Jeffreys, 2018), but it provides support for Wagenaar's

(2017) idea of 'authentic dialogue' and suggests a working model for how we can move debates about sex work forward.

6.4 Conclusion

The career development programs we highlight in this chapter show the potential that exists for these services when they adopt a career development framework. The meaningful involvement of marginalised voices and communities in policymaking and research is not a new concept; however, this is not always applied when it comes to working with sex workers (Garofalo Geymonat & Macioti, 2016; SWAN, 2019). NUM and Respect Inc show that when support is designed by and for sex workers and is evidence-based, services can be tailored to the diverse experiences and social identities within the sex industry, while also supporting the idea that services do not need to be conditional on people leaving or staying in sex work. The programs featured in this chapter were not based on rescue models or diversion framings, nor did they make judgements about sex work and sex workers, instead, there were diverse opportunities for empowerment and skill development, with services embedded in sex worker rights advocacy and activism and located in a career framing. They show what is possible when sex work is reconfigured within a career framework, and this means the ability to recognise the diversity of sex work careers and the broader socio-economic and cultural forces shaping career choices. These forces are often ignored in deviance and victimhood framings that shape public policy and programs, which gives further support for the need to reconfigure 'exiting' as career development.

In this chapter, we have shifted the framing of 'exiting' by adopting a career lens, in contrast to previous studies, therefore presenting a new way of theorising about the issue. This allowed us to propose an alternative way of thinking about 'exiting' and challenge the status quo based on grounded realities and experiences. It also demonstrates the importance and value of researching and developing policy with sex workers rather than on sex workers (Aroney & Crofts, 2019; Connelly & Sanders, 2020). We have also shown that debates about sex work are not just the preserve of academics, for as Connelly and Sanders remind us, they:

> … inform real-life tussles in politics, policy and everyday practice. Sex workers generally, and sex workers who are activists particularly, grapple

with the issues central to these debates (some would say life and death issues) on a daily basis (2020, p. 204).

This chapter has documented sex workers' efforts to disrupt and challenge some of the harmful narratives about the sex industry, and create policies and programs developed by sex workers, for sex workers. Through this, we have been able to present a more complex picture able to account for "the ways in which career decisions and economic outcomes are affected by social roles; the impact of the broader gendered labour market on individual career decisions; as well as the ways in which individuals negotiate structural barriers in order to carve out their careers" in sex work (Gilmour, 2020, p. 310). We have shown how this can challenge dominant ideas about sex workers as victims in need of protection or deviants who need to be controlled or punished. It also elucidates how, and why, we can and should understand sex work as skilled labour. The stereotype of sex workers being trapped in the industry and sex work as purely harm says more about how sex workers have been constructed as unruly subjects than it speaks of their lived experiences, diverse knowledges and possibilities. It is a framing that ignores the significant contribution sex workers and sex worker advocates have made to improving policy development, transforming understandings of and attitudes towards sex work and sex workers and enhancing their safety and well-being.

References

Aroney, E., & Crofts, P. (2019). How sex worker activism influenced the decriminalisation of sex work in NSW, Australia. *International Journal for Crime, Justice and Social Democracy, 8*(2), 50–67. https://doi.org/10.5204/ijcjsd.v8i2.955

Baratosy, R., & Wendt, S. (2017). "Outdated laws, outspoken whores": Exploring sex work in a criminalised setting. *Women's Studies International Forum, 62*, 34–42. https://doi.org/10.1016/j.wsif.2017.03.002

Benoit, C., & Mellor, A. (2023). Decriminalization and what else? Alternative structural interventions to promote the health, safety and rights of sex workers. *Social Sciences, 12*, 202. https://doi.org/10.3390/socsci12040202

Bowen, R. (2021). *Work, money and duality: Trading sex as a side hustle*. Bristol University Press.

BSI Learning. (2013a). *Reducing recidivism rates by changing mindset through the P2Eprogram*. Online: http://www.bsilearning.edu.au/case-studies/client-queensland-correctional-services

BSI Learning. (2013b). *Career transition program.* Online: http://www.bsilearning.edu.au/blog/item/139-career-transition-program

BSI Learning. (2013c). *Case study - BSI learning case managers change the mindset and lives of women who previously thought there was no way out of their dangerous lifestyle.* Online: http://www.bsilearning.edu.au/case-studies/client-hope-foundation

Chan, D. (1999. September). *Trafficking and prostitution* [Paper presentation]. First national conference on gender and development 1999, Phnom Penh, Cambodia.

Connelly, L., & Sanders, T. (2020). Disrupting the boundaries of the academe: Co-creating knowledge and sex work 'academic-activism'. In S. Walklate, K. FitzGibbon, J. McCulloch, & J. Maher (Eds.), *The Emerald handbook of feminism, criminology and social change* (pp. 203–218).

Crime and Misconduct Commission (CMC). (2011). *Emerald Regulating prostitution: A follow-up review of the Prostitution Act 1999.* Crime and Misconduct Commission. Online:https://www.ccc.qld.gov.au/sites/default/files/Docs/Publications/CMC/Regulating-prostitution-A-follow-up-review-of-the-Prostitution-Act-1999-%28QLD%29-Report-2011.pdf

CMC. (2004). *Regulating prostitution: An evaluation of the Prostitution Act 1999 (QLD).* Crime and Misconduct Commission. Online: https://www.ccc.qld.gov.au/sites/default/files/Docs/Publications/CMC/Regulating-prostitution-An-Evaluation-of-the-Prostitution-Act-1999-%28QLD%29-Report-2004.pdf

Garofalo Geymonat, G., & Macioti, P. G. (2016). Sex workers speak: Who listens? In G. Garofalo Geymonat & P. G. Macioti (Eds.), *Sex workers speak. Who listens?* (pp. 1–10). Cost Action & University of Essex.

Gilmour, F. (2020). Careers in the Australian sex industry: Exploring life narratives through metaphor. *Journal of Sociology, 56*(3), 297–313. https://doi.org/10.1177/1440783319893462

Greenhaus, J., & Callanan, G. (2006). *Encyclopedia of career development*. Sage.

Ham, J., & Gilmour, F. (2016). 'We all have one': Exit plans as a professional strategy in sex work. *Work, Employment and Society, 31*(5), 748–763. https://doi.org/10.1177/0950017016666198

Hester, M., & Westmarland, N. (2004). *Tackling street prostitution: Towards an holistic approach.* Home Office Research Studies.

Jeffreys, E. (2018). Public encounters with whorephobia: Making sense of hostility toward sex worker advocates. In S. Dewey, I. Crowhurst, & C. Izugbara (Eds.), *Routledge international handbook of sex industry research* (pp. 761–776). Routledge.

McKewon, E. (2005). *The scarlet mile: A social history of prostitution in Kalgoorlie*, 1894-2004. University of Western Australia Publishing

Maher, J., Pickering, S., & Gerard, A. (2012). Privileging work not sex: Flexibility and employment in the sexual services industry. *The Sociological Review, 60*, 546–675. https://doi.org/10.1111/j.1467-954X.2012.02128.x

National Ugly Mugs (NUM). (2025). *Vocational support services.* Online: https://nationaluglymugs.org/vocational-support/#WORKshops

NUM. (2022). *Leaving the game: Research on sex work, mainstream work and more.* Online: https://nationaluglymugs.org/2022/07/28/leaving-the-game-research-on-sex-work-mainstream-work-and-mo

Overs, C. (2020). *Decriminalisation in Victoria: Reasons for optimism.* Online: https://swvoicesvic.com/articles/decriminalisation-in-victoria-reasons-for-optimism/

Platt, L., Grenfell, P., Meiksin, R., Elmes, J., Sherman, S., Sanders, T., MwangiI, P., & Crago, A. (2018). Associations between sex work laws and sex workers' health: A systematic review and meta-analysis of quantitative and qualitative studies. *PLoS Medicine, 15*(12), 1–54. https://doi.org/10.1371/journal.Pmed.1002680

Pickering, S., Maher, J., & Gerard, A. (2009). *Working in Victorian brothels: An independent report commissioned by consumer affairs Victoria into the Victorian brothel sector.* Monash University.

Respect Inc. (2023). *Career development program.* Online: https://respectqld.org.au/drop-in/cdp/

Respect Inc. (2021). *Respect Inc—who are we?* Online: https://respectqld.org.au/what-is-respect-inc/

Rowe, J. (2011). *SHANTUSI: Surveying HIV and need in the unregulated sex industry*. Inner South Community Health & RMIT University.

Sandy, L. (2000). *"It's all too public": Policy formation on the sex industry in Western Australia* [Honours dissertation, Curtin University].

Sandy, L. (2014). *Women and sex work in Cambodia: Blood, sweat and tears.* Routledge.

Sandy, L., Meenagh, J., & Nes-Iadicola, P. (2019). *Transitioning programs for sex workers: An exploration of promising practice. Technical and background paper.* RMIT University.

Sandy, L., & Matthews, D. (2025). *Can we improve trust in the police? How adaptations to police liaison program models can improve sex worker safety.* Institute of Policy and Engagement Policy Brief. University of Nottingham. Online: https://www.nottingham.ac.uk/policy-and-engagement/documents/policy-briefs/larissa-sandy-can-we-improve-trust-in-the-police.pdf

Scarlet Alliance. (2024). *Sex work laws in Australia.* Online: https://scarletalliance.org.au/resources/laws/

The Sex Workers' Rights Advocacy Network (SWAN). (2019). *Nothing about us without us! A brief guide on meaningful involvement of sex workers and their organisations in Central Eastern Europe and Central Asia (CEECA)*. Online: https://swannet.org/resources/nothing-about-us-without-us-a-brief-guide-on-meaningful-involvement-of-sex-workers-and-their-organisations-in-central-eastern-europe-and-central-asia/

Sullivan, B. (2003). Trafficking in women. *International Feminist Journal of Politics, 5*(1), 67–91. https://doi.org/10.1080/1461674021000056773

Wagenaar, H. (2017). Why prostitution policy (usually) fails and what to do about it? *Social Sciences, 6*(2), 43. https://doi.org/10.3390/socsci6020043

Wagenaar, H., & Altink, S. (2012). Prostitution as morality politics or why it is exceedingly difficult to design and sustain effective prostitution policy. *Sexuality Research and Social Policy, 9*, 279–292. https://doi.org/10.1007/s13178-012-0095-0

Wallace Lockhart, D. (2025). Sex worker 'terrified' by plans for new prostitution law. *BBC News*. Online: https://www.bbc.co.uk/news/articles/cx2xwlxrq4lo

World Health Organization (WHO). (1986). *The Ottawa charter*. WHO. Online: https://www.who.int/publications/i/item/WH-1987

Legislation Cited

Criminal Code (Decriminalising Sex Work) and Other Legislation Amendment Bill (Queensland) (2024).

Prostitution Act (Queensland) (1999).

Sex Industry Act (Northern Territory) (2019).

Sex Industry Offences Act (Tasmania) (2005).

Sex Work Act (Australian Capital Territory) (1992).

Sex Work Decriminalisation Act (Victoria) (2022).

Summary Offences Act (South Australia) (1953).

CHAPTER 7

Conclusion

Abstract This chapter draws together the key themes of the book and spells out the importance of reconceptualising 'exiting' as career development as part of a new framework presented in the book. In using sex work as career to redefine 'exiting', we show how this can extend understandings of sex work as work and offer an alternative perspective to the abolitionist, mostly Western radical feminist view that dominates international debates. This can result in a paradigm shift, transforming sex work 'exiting' from something sex workers need to stop doing to sex work careers, analysed from the lives, agency, rights, voices and views of diverse peoples engaged in sex work. In this way, we link theory and practice in ways previously overlooked by researchers and academics to design a new framework that can create greater social acceptance of sex work as work and lead to changes in policy and practice. We also make a case for societal change by discussing the paradox of 'exiting': this area of programming claims to help workers but, as we argue, it is achieved at the cost of further compounding marginalisation and reinforcing harms, while simultaneously acting as a domain of oppression in their lives. Finally, we argue for the pressing need to include sex workers in the development of research, policy and programs and see this as a way to shift policy stagnation and challenge the morality politics and punitive and paternalistic responses to sex work and sex workers that perpetuate stigmatisation and marginalisation.

L. Sandy et al., *Reconceptualizing Exiting and Career Development in Sex Work*, Palgrave Advances in Sex Work Studies,
https://doi.org/10.1007/978-3-032-10077-1_7

Keywords Sex work · Career development · Stigma · Decriminalisation · Agency

7.1 Conclusion

This book has grappled with the question of how to conceptualise, and accordingly, how to respond to 'exiting'. We have covered diverse agendas and ideas about gender equality, exploitation, sex work regulation and the regulation of sexuality to self-determination, working conditions, socio-economic disparities, labour market dynamics and careers in sex work. We have probed the place of 'exiting' in sex work and ultimately reached the conclusion that the focus of regulatory approaches that criminalise sex work as deviance or exploitation drive debate and discussion towards bodies and sex rather than working conditions and employment (Maher et al., 2012). This book is part of ongoing efforts to theorise sex work as labour, and in it we have raised, and answered crucial questions about the place of 'exiting' in labour frameworks. Exit planning in sex work can offer benefit in shaping a "strategic and focused approach" to work and enabling transitions (Ham & Gilmour, 2016, p. 761). By exploring everyday practices and sex workers' realities, we put forward a new framework reconceptualising 'exiting' sex work as career and understanding this as part of career development or transitions. In unearthing sex workers' resistance to this area of programming, we presented some very compelling reasons for this paradigm shift while exploring the power and politics of 'exiting'. We have shown how the dominant framework shaping 'exiting' programs is part of the stigmatising and harmful language, discourse and practices sex workers are subject to:

> … it's a different story when [people] … are specifically using language as a tactic to oppress you. Sex work is work. My work is real and I have never had anyone adequately explain how having less rights would somehow 'save me' or improve my situation (Green, 2015, para 24).

The language used in 'exiting' discourse stigmatises and marginalises sex workers. As Lexxie Jury passionately argued, it is time we changed the narrative, and on this we agree. We have shown how and where 'exiting' may and may not fit with sex workers' narratives and lived experiences, and this grounded approach elucidates how public discourse on 'exiting' has become emotionalised with policies and programs designed around emotions and not evidence (Freiberg & Carson, 2010). In doing so, we have challenged the discourse surrounding sex work categorisations as either 'involved' or 'exited', and the prevailing view of these categories being distinct and stable (Aylsworth, 2020). Clearly, this is not the case as we have shown how sex workers' experiences are diverse, multifaceted, complex, evolving and fluid.

In our exploration of the dominant frameworks shaping conceptualisations of 'exiting', we highlighted how, while they might favour deviance or see sex work purely as harm, the approaches are all accompanied by regulatory environments that feature criminalisation. We argued that this then obscures an understanding of labour market conditions, worker participation and non-participation decisions and career framings. Here we suggest that, while the focus on harm and stigma is necessary, this can come at the expense of understanding the importance of working conditions and flexibility. It can also impede understanding the centrality of these factors in worker's decision-making, career planning and individual and collective agency and the interplay between social and structural factors. It also comes at the cost of considering language, and the need to continually challenge terms like 'exiting' as harmful and reinforcing stigma.

Career development in sex work is an area of service delivery where programs and options need to be tailored to suit individual needs and address the diversity among sex workers and in the sex industry. Some services may support sex workers' various goals and identities, but conversely, these may not suit others, for example religiously orientated services—the research shows some value in these services for religious sex workers and how they offer holistic support. These specialist faith-based organisations are important as they can offer faith-based support that secular organisations may not be able to provide for religious sex workers; however, this service provision needs to be non-judgmental. For other sex workers, they may need intensive case management and support while others might prefer a community-based approach—there is no one-size-fits-all approach that can address diverse needs. It is vitally important we ensure sex workers can access the right services for them and their needs, and at a time and place that is best for them. At the same time, these services need to be non-judgemental and here we need to challenge stigma and discrimination and framings of sex work as morally wrong in most 'exiting' programs.

In our discussions, we explored the harms emanating from seeing sex workers as either deviants or victims or both: seeing sex workers through a singular identity leads to programs that fail workers. This is because the program either focuses on reducing crime, with sex workers being granted a chance to 'turn their life around', or as victims of exploitation and violence, they are rescued from a terrible, chaotic life of exploitation and abuse. This does not mean we found no elements of good practice in the case studies presented in Chapter 3. Here, we argued that, while the aims and ethos of these programs were problematic, some sex workers did benefit from them. However, until these services are sex worker-led, and at the very least, offer holistic non-judgemental support and are not shaped by an ulterior motive of removing sex workers from the industry and abolishing sex work, they remain limited and will continue to reinforce harm to sex workers. In contrast, Chapter 6 detailed the possibilities of career development programs when they demonstrate promising practice, which included seeing sex work as work, adopting a rights-based approach and community empowerment framework, peer driven (sex worker-led), and offering peer engagement and outreach. These programs did not focus on supporting workers to 'exit' the industry, rather they supported sex workers to fulfil their goals and helped in navigating barriers they faced due to stigma and other factors.

Our analyses revealed the need for career development programs because of sex work stigma and criminalisation; however, this need centres around societies coming to understand the valuable skillset sex workers have, which includes, but is certainly not limited to advertising, communications, rapport building, financial management, business planning and so on. Understanding sex work as career helps us comprehend the vast range of skills needed in sex work and challenges the prevailing idea that sex workers need help to leave the industry because they have no skills, training and experiences or that sex work is the only occupation they know. It also challenges the framing of sex work as a dead-end job in most 'exiting' research. Here, our analyses and research have filled a significant gap in the literature by presenting the diverse voices and views of sex workers that underscored the problematic framings of respectability in 'exiting'. This discourse of respectability in sex work 'exiting' reinforces societal ideas that sex work and sex workers are not legitimate. Hence, the context 'exiting' programs operate in is one where sex work is seen as 'unworthy work' and sex workers as 'unworthy subjects'. Ultimately, as unrespectable and unruly subjects, the 'exiting' industry exists as part of societal attempts to make sex workers 'respectable subjects'. Respectability, then, becomes the reason for the 'exiting' industry and this is why some sex workers object to, and reject these programs. Instead, we have shown what is possible when sex work is seen as skilled work, and 'exiting' is reconceptualised as career development and the role this can play in reducing stigma and discrimination.

The ideas about sex work and sex workers in 'exiting' discourse must be challenged for we have shown how this leads to viewing sex workers as subjects without value and this can operate as a domain of oppression in their lives. Our exploration of labour market practices in Chapters 5 and 6 mounted a powerful challenge against the orthodoxy. In these chapters, we showed how some sex workers strategically used 'exit planning' to shape their careers in sex work in the short, medium and long term. Exploring labour market practices and conditions enabled us to show how wider employment options and working patterns may not work for some people, particularly women and other marginalised and racialised groups. In following Maher, Pickering and Gerard (2012), our analyses have shown how sex work flexibility, and sex workers' employment security needs to be part of discussions about sex work and career planning. This was key in understanding how social and economic constraints interacted with poor working conditions in broader labour markets to shape and influence careers in sex work.

We have shown how understanding sex work as career is fundamental in reconceptualising 'exiting' as career development. More importantly, we have demonstrated why this conceptual change is important: employment rights and working conditions need to be a key focus in sex work debates and regulations. As Maher, Pickering and Gerard argue, "discussions about sex work as work and workers' security must be in the context of the general labour market conditions that militate against equitable employment for many [people], especially those undertaking care responsibilities or managing education costs" for others or while undertaking their own studies (2012, p. 672). We have shown how a labour market framing can help us make sense of sex workers' choices and career decisions. However, it is imperative that the focus on autonomy and self-determination goes beyond individualised models of personal choice to consider the "terrain of agency in circumstances in which social and economic constraints restrict the freedom to choose" viable alternatives

(Munro & Della Giusta, 2008, p. 4, see also Sandy, 2014). The research we document shows how some sex workers navigate career decisions where the wages and flexibility offered in sex work outweigh the poor wages and conditions in other areas of the labour market. It exemplifies how the organisation of labour markets across societies more generally fails to allow for the full and equal participation of all groups, particularly women and other marginalised, stigmatised and racialised groups (Bowen, 2021; Gilmour, 2020; Maher et al., 2012). Using a sex work as work lens and career framing means that we can ensure workers' rights and conditions are protected in programs, services and policies and addressed in research.

In addition to the punitive measures governing sex work and negative moral judgements made about it, we have shown how "many sex workers have a history of complexity in their lives that predisposes them to comparatively high degrees of food insecurity and other forms of economic hardship, low educational achievement, inadequate housing, poor physical and mental health, high levels of long-term disability and unmet health needs, and elevated rates of assault and victimization" (Benoit & Mellor, 2023, p. 203). Career development programs, then, need to adopt an intersectional lens and consider structural interventions alongside the need for social and legal reform to improve sex workers' lives and reduce harm. We have shown the importance of ensuring that programs accommodate diversity in sex workers' lives and experiences and varied needs based on working locations, life circumstances, social positioning and future aspirations. We evidenced examples of this in the person-centred programs developed as part of sex worker-led interventions like Respect Inc's *Career Development Program* and NUM's *Work! Work! Work! Vocational Support Program*. These programs also show us how "'care' can be nuanced in relation to the needs and experiences of sex workers, and the multiple dimensions of this, including self, community, collective, and accountability-related care" as well as care in careers and career development (Benoit & Mellor, 2023, p. 204; see also Mellor et al., 2025; NUM, 2022; Sitter et al., 2022).

Through the idea of sex work as work and careers in sex work, we can shift 'exiting' beyond the highly individualised focus on specialist case management and the in/out binary that holds sway to consider macro-, meso- and micro-level interventions to improve sex workers' welfare and employment opportunities inside and outside of the sex industry. Indeed, by centring sex workers voices, we can challenge and disrupt stigmatising narratives aimed at marginalising sex workers in 'exiting' discourse. It is important our work and efforts in this space challenge the idea of homogeneity (i.e., sex workers as cis women who are sexually exploited). More research is needed to document the diversity among sex workers, which the literature has largely failed to be capture. We have highlighted significant gaps in research. Firstly, we have illustrated how sex workers' diverse experiences are mostly absent from the picture, and this means that policy and programs, and theoretical frameworks will continue to fail. Secondly, while sex work is relatively over-researched, very little studies have included the vast majority of sex workers. To date, the 'exiting' literature has almost exclusively focused on street-based cis women working in the industry. This means we have almost no research with men who sex work, queer sex workers, gay sex workers (including women and men), trans sex workers, asexual sex workers, bi and pansexual sex workers, migrant and racialised sex workers, gender diverse and non-binary sex workers, workers with a disability or people working in different sectors of the industry like stripping, massage, escort, BDSM/fetish or kink practitioners and so on. A small number of studies have included indoor and online workers, but more research is needed if we are to develop grounded theory and evidence-based policies in this area. Given the problematic nature and contested terrain of 'exiting' research, this work must be carried out in partnership with sex workers and sex worker organisations. It is important for research to explore the vital role that sex worker support organisations play in providing safe spaces for people doing sex work and facilitating access to health and social services and vocational support. Finally, more research is needed to document practices and build the evidence base, but more importantly in building on the work of Mellor et al. (2025), Sandy et al. (2019), and Sitter et al. (2022) that establishes evidence-based good practice, this research needs to be extended to develop an accountability care framework with sex workers.

As Benoit and Mellor note, "people who sell sexual services have historically experienced marginalization across multiple domains of oppression, facing restricted access to key resources to support their safety at work, economic security, and overall quality of life" (2023, p. 206). This book has highlighted the paradox of 'exiting' revealing how this area of programming compounds marginalisation and acts as a domain of oppression, while claiming to do the exact opposite. We have identified a need for services and support for sex workers in this area, but this need is largely due to stigma and discrimination and criminalisation as well as enhancing sex workers' health and improving safety, and for this, we need a change in focus from 'exiting' to career development. Career development programs can also address economic precarity and work to challenge social and political inequalities and reduce stigma.

Sex work 'exiting' is an area where issues of morality and innocence have dominated for too long (Kantola & Squires, 2004). We have shown how the involvement of sex workers and sex worker organisations in 'authentic dialogue' (Wagenaar, 2017) with researchers has been a pathway to shifting the ideology driven approaches in 'exiting'—here we invited and listened to sex workers' critiques and co-collaborated in developing a novel, grounded framework to guide research and practice and overcome stagnation. Moreover, we have proposed a framework for authentic dialogue in 'exiting' research involving epistemic, social and compassionate foundations (Choi, 2014), and here, by paying attention to the emotional component of this, we uncovered and revealed sex worker resistance and developed a new conceptual framework as part of the collective goal of sex work decriminalisation and ending stigma and discrimination.

References

Aylsworth, L. (2020). *Rethinking 'involvement' in sex work: Examining sex workers relationship with sex work* [doctoral dissertation, University of Alberta]. *ERA*. https://era.library.ualberta.ca/items/678db113-4e1a-45d7-b338-36969ed2f358

Benoit, C., & Mellor, A. (2023). Decriminalization and what else? Alternative structural interventions to promote the health, safety, and rights of sex workers. *Social Sciences, 12*(4), 202. https://doi.org/10.3390/socsci12040202

Bowen, R. (2021). *Work, money and duality: Trading sex as a side hustle*. Bristol University Press.

Freiberg, A., & Carson, W. (2010). The limits to evidence-based policy: Evidence, emotion and criminal justice. *The Australian Journal of Public Administration, 69*(2), 152–164. https://doi.org/10.1111/j.1467-8500.2010.00674.x

Choi, T. (2014). Rational and compassionate information processing: A conceptual framework for authentic dialogue. *Public Administration Review, 74*(6), 726–735. https://doi.org/10.1111/puar.12277

Gilmour, F. (2020). Careers in the Australian sex industry: Exploring life narratives through metaphor. *Journal of Sociology, 56*(3), 297–313. https://doi.org/10.1177/1440783319893462

Green, J. (2015, 12 August). Forum on regulating sex work in Western Australia. *Sexliesducttape.* https://sexliesducttape.me/2015/08/12/forum-on-regulating-sex-work-in-western-australia/

Ham, J., & Gilmour, F. (2016). 'We all have one': Exit plans as a professional strategy in sex work. *Work, Employment and Society, 31*(5), 748–763. https://doi.org/10.1177/0950017016666198

Kantola, J., & Squires, J. (2004). Discourses surrounding prostitution policies in the UK. *European Journal of Women's Studies, 11*(1), 77–101. https://doi.org/10.1177/1350506804039815

Maher, J., Pickering, S., & Gerard, A. (2012). Privileging work not sex: Flexibility and employment in the sexual services industry. *The Sociological Review, 60*, 546–675. https://doi.org/10.1111/j.1467-954X.2012.02128.x

Mellor, A., Benoit, C., & Koenig, B. (2025). Ecological contexts of resilience in sex work: Managing a precarious, stigmatized and criminalized occupation in one Canadian city. *Sexes, 6*(1), 11. https://doi.org/10.3390/sexes6010011

Munro, V., & Della Giusta, M. (2008). The regulation of prostitution: Contemporary contexts and comparative perspectives. In V. Munro & M. Della Giusta (Eds.), *Demanding sex: Critical reflections on the regulation of prostitution* (pp. 1–12). Ashgate.

National Ugly Mugs (NUM). (2022). *Leaving the game: Research on sex work, mainstream work and more.* Online: https://nationaluglymugs.org/2022/07/28/leaving-the-game-research-on-sex-work-mainstream-work-and-mo

Sandy, L. (2014). *Women and sex work in Cambodia: Blood, sweat and tears.* Routledge.

Sandy, L., Meenagh, J., & Nes-Iadicola, P. (2019). *Transitioning programs for sex workers: An exploration of promising practice.* RMIT University.

Sitter, K., Grittner, A., Pabia, M., & Jarvis, H. (2022). "We knew no one else had our back except us": Recommendations for creating an accountability care framework with sex workers in eastern Canada. *Social Sciences, 11*(8), 366. https://doi.org/10.3390/socsci11080366

Wagenaar, H. (2017). Why prostitution policy (usually) fails and what to do about it? *Social Sciences, 6*(2), 43. https://doi.org/10.3390/socsci6020043

Index

L. Sandy et al., *Reconceptualizing Exiting and Career Development in Sex Work*, Palgrave Advances in Sex Work Studies,
https://doi.org/10.1007/978-3-032-10077-1

FSC
www.fsc.org
MIX
Papier | Fördert gute Waldnutzung
FSC® C083411

Kolibri 360 GmbH
Ferdinand-Jühlke-Straße 7
99095 Erfurt, Deutschland
produktsicherheit@kolibri360.de